Law with a personal touch

Doing Business in Russia

Brief Legal Guide

4th edition

Edited by Vladimir Kilinkarov and Maxim Avrashkov
Maxima Legal LLC, Russia

2016

УДК 334(470+571)+347.1(470+571)
ББК 65.9(2Рос)09+67.404(2Рос)
D65

DOING BUSINESS IN RUSSIA	BRIEF LEGAL GUIDE
ST. PETERSBURG	2016

Edited by Vladimir Kilinkarov and Maxim Avrashkov

Written by Maxim Avrashkov, Sergey Bakeshin, Evgeny Druzhinin, Vladimir Kilinkarov, Elena Kilinkarova, Alina Kozmina, Karina Starikova, Artur Osipov and Natalia Zelentsova

Doing Business in Russia : Brief Legal Guide /edited by Vladimir Kilinkarov and Maxim Avrashkov.– St. Petersburg : Russian Collection, 2015. - 172 p.

I. Kilinkarov, Vladimir, ред. - 1.

This is the 4th edition of the Maxima Legal guide to the principal legal aspects of conducting business in Russia. The handbook offers a brief overview of key elements of the Russian legal regulation covering corporations, contracts, tax, M&A, customs, real estate & construction, public regulation, PPP, WTO, immigration, employment, intellectual property, protection of competition, insolvency and dispute resolution. The book is recommended to foreign businessmen working or planning to develop their business in Russia, lawyers, and anybody who would like to know more about the Russian legal system and relevant requirements for doing business in Russia.

All information presented in the handbook has been thoroughly revised and updated to reflect the last amendments to the Russian legislation (up to the 01 May, 2015) as well as the most actual draft amendments, acts and trendlines in certain areas of Russian law.

Published by RBO Books © 2016
Distributed by Glagoslav Publications Ltd. © 2016

ISBN 978-5-901440-82-7 (RU)
ISBN 978-1-78437-969-8 (UK)

© Group of authors, 2016
© Maxima Legal LLC, 2016

Dear Friends!

This is the 4th edition of the guide to the principal legal aspects of conducting business in Russia. It has been written by practicing lawyers of Maxima Legal LLC for foreign businessmen working or planning to develop their business in Russia, lawyers, and anybody who would like to know more about the Russian legal system and relevant requirements for doing business in Russia.

The guide offers a brief overview of key elements of the Russian legal regulation covering corporations, contracts, tax, M&A, customs, real estate & construction, public regulation, PPP, WTO, immigration, employment, intellectual property, protection of competition, insolvency and dispute resolution. We recommend this information to anybody who has business in Russia or plans to do so in future.

All information presented in the handbook has been thoroughly revised and updated to reflect the last amendments to the Russian legislation (up to the 01 May, 2015) as well as the most actual draft amendments, acts and prospects in different areas of Russian law.

Should you have any questions or wish to obtain additional information on any issue, please feel free to contact us. Our contact information is listed at the end of this brochure.

We hope you will find this information interesting and useful.

With kind regards,

Maxim Avrashkov and Vladimir Kilinkarov
Maxima Legal LLC

Contents

General Information

* by Maxim Avrashkov, Natalia Zelentsova

Background information:

* Russia (the Russian Federation) is the largest country in the world;
* Russia is located in Eastern Europe and Northern Asia;
* the population of Russia is around 146 million people;
* Russia borders 18 countries (more than any other country); it has land borders with the following countries: Norway, Finland, Estonia, Latvia, Lithuania, Poland, Belarus, Ukraine, Abkhazia, Georgia, South Ossetia, Azerbaijan, Kazakhstan, China, Mongolia and North Korea; it has sea frontiers (only) with Japan and the USA;
* after the collapse of the USSR in late 1991, the Russian Federation was recognized by the international community as the successor state to the Union of Soviet Socialist Republics;
* Russia's principal foreign trade partners are Germany, China, the Netherlands, Italy, Ukraine, Belarus, Cyprus, Turkey, Poland, the USA, the United Kingdom, Kazakhstan, France, Switzerland and Finland;
* Russia has the world's largest mineral and energy reserves; the country is extremely rich in such mineral resources as oil, natural gas, coal, iron, gold *etc*. Russia is the world leader in forest area (45% of the country's territory); it possesses approximately 1/5 of the world's timber resources. Russia has the world's largest number of lakes, which contain around one quarter of the world's resources of unfrozen fresh water. Land and other natural resources are used and protected in the Russian Federation as fundamentals of the life and activities of peoples living in the respective territory;
* the capital of Russia is Moscow. There are 14 Russian cities with a population of over one million people: Moscow, St. Petersburg, Novosibirsk, Yekaterinburg, Nizhny Novgorod, Kazan, Samara, Omsk, Chelyabinsk, Rostov-on-Don and Ufa, Volgograd, Perm, Krasnoyarsk;
* the official currency of Russia is the ruble.

Fundamentals of the Constitutional System

The principal law of the Russian state is the **Constitution of the Russian Federation**. The **RF Constitution** has supreme force in law, directly affecting and applying to the entire territory of Russia. The RF Constitution secures the fundamentals of the constitutional system of the Russian Federation, human and civil rights and liberties, a federal form of government, and the organization of the supreme bodies of state authority.

The official language of Russia is Russian. Peoples of the Russian Federation are guaranteed the right to preserve their native tongue. Russia is a multinational country. In this connection, the organization of national policy (a system of measures focused on the renewal and further evolution of the national life of all peoples of Russia within the framework of a federal state, and establishment of equitable relations between the country's peoples, the formation of democratic mechanisms for resolving national and interethnic problems) is of paramount importance.

The Russian Federation is a secular state. No religion may be proclaimed official or mandatory. The most popular religion is Orthodox Christianity; residents of multinational Russia also profess Islam, Catholicism, Judaism and Buddhism.

Russia is a democratic federal law-based state with a republican (presidential) form of government.

The constitutional system in Russia, including state and political systems, is determined by the Constitution of the Russian Federation, adopted by a nationwide vote on 12 December 1993.

In defining the fundamentals of the constitutional system in Russia, Article 2 of the RF Constitution states the basic provision that the individual, his/her rights and liberties are of paramount value, and that the recognition, observation and protection of these rights and liberties is the obligation of the state. Human rights and liberties may be restricted in exceptional circumstances stipulated in federal law.

For the first time, the country's constitutional legislation expressly states that it is directly oriented on internationally recognized principles of the regulation of human rights and liberties and acknowledgment of the natural and innate character of basic human rights and liberties, including the right to life, freedom and personal security, the right to privacy, the right to respect for private and family life, the right to protection of honor, dignity and good reputation, the right to private property, the right to freedom of thought and the right to a favorable environment. Human and civil rights in the Russian Federation are universal. No constituent territory of the Russian Federation may decline the obligation to observe and guarantee human and civil rights on its territory. No law or other legislative act may contradict the human and civil rights secured by the RF Constitution.

The Universal Declaration of Human Rights (1948), the International Covenant on Civil and Political Rights (1966), the International Covenant on Economic, Social and Cultural Rights (1996) and the European Convention for the Protection of Human Rights and Fundamental Freedoms (1950) are effective in Russia.

In order to emphasize the role and importance of constitutional human and civil rights and liberties, Article 18 of the RF Constitution states that they have direct effect and determine the meaning, content and application of laws, the activities of legislative and executive authorities and local government, and are guaranteed by law. The provision of the direct application of the said rights and liberties means that they must be granted with direct reference to the RF Constitution, irrespective of the presence or absence of other legislation, and in the event of a breach thereof any person may defend them in court, referring to the principle of direct application of the RF Constitution.

The RF Constitution determines that international law shall prevail over national law. According to Part 4 of Article 15 of the RF Constitution, the generally recognized principles and regulations of international law and international agreements to which the Russian Federation is a party are a constituent part of its legal system. If an international agreement to which the Russian Federation is a party establishes rules that differ from those specified by law, the rules of the international agreement shall apply.

The Russian Federation is a social country whose policy is aimed at the creation of the conditions for a decent life and free development for each person. In the Russian Federation people's employment and health is protected, a minimum salary is guaranteed, state protection is provided for the family, maternity, paternity and childhood, handicapped people and senior citizens, a system of social services is developed, and state pensions, allowances and other social security guarantees are established.

Unity of the economic area, free transfer of commodities, services and funds, support of competition and freedom of economic activity are guaranteed in Russia.

Private, state, municipal and other forms of property are equally recognized and protected in the Russian Federation.

Ideological and political diversity and pluralism are recognized in the Russian Federation.

State Structure

State authority in the Russian Federation is divided into legislative authority, executive authority and judicial authority. Legislative, executive and judicial bodies are independent, but there is a system of checks and balances.

State authority in the Russian federation is exercised by the President of the Russian Federation, the Federal Assembly (the Federal Council and the State Duma), the Government of the Russian Federation and the courts of the Russian Federation. State authority in constituent territories of the Russian Federation is exercised by organs of state power formed by them. Demarcation of competence and powers between the state authorities of the Russian Federation and the state authorities of constituent territories of the Russian Federation is established by means of the RF Constitution, Federal (or other) Agreements on the Demarcation of Competence and Powers.

Local government is recognized and guaranteed in the Russian Federation. Local governments are independent within the scope of their authority. Local government authorities are not part of the system of state authorities.

The Head of State is the **President of Russia**, elected for a six-year term (four years prior to 2008) by means of a nationwide election. In accordance with the current Constitution, he exercises a number of important powers: he is in charge of foreign policy, is the Supreme Commander-in-Chief of the Armed Forces, appoints the Prime Minister with the consent of the State Duma and accepts resolutions for the resignation of the Government. On the proposal of the Prime Minister, the President of Russia appoints and dismisses Deputy Prime Ministers and federal ministers. The President of Russia is Head of the Security Council, and appoints and dismisses the command the Armed Forces. He has the right to propose nominees for the post of Chairman of the

Central Bank (not included in the Government structure). In the event of aggression or an immediate threat of aggression, the President is entitled to declare martial law in the entire country or in individual territories, but is obliged to notify the Federal Assembly of his decision immediately. The President is entitled to issue decrees that are binding for the whole of Russia (these decrees may not contradict federal laws).

The President may be dismissed by the Federal Council if he has been accused by the State Duma of treason or other serious offenses and in the event of him being found guilty by the Supreme and Constitutional Courts.

Legislative authority is exercised by the Federal Assembly, a parliament consisting of two houses: the Federal Council (the Upper House) and the State Duma (the Lower House). Two representatives of each constituent territory of the Russian Federation shall be the members of the Federal Council: one representative from the representative body of state authority and one representative from the executive body of state authority. The State Duma consists of 450 deputies elected in the course of a nationwide election according to party lists for a term of 5 years.

Executive authority is exercised by the Government of the Russian Federation. The Government of the Russian Federation consists of the Prime Minister of the Russian Federation, Deputy Prime Ministers of the Russian Federation and federal ministers. The system of federal bodies of the executive authority includes federal ministries, federal services and federal agencies.

Judicial authority is exercised by the courts: the Constitutional Court, courts of general jurisdiction and arbitration (commercial) courts headed by the Supreme Court. Constitutional (statutory) courts are established in some constituent territories of the Russian Federation, where the judicial system also includes Justices of the Peace. The setting up of emergency courts is not permitted. In accordance with the RF Constitution, justice may be dispensed only by a court.

Federal Form of Government

Russia is a state with a federal form of government. The Russian Federation consists of republics, territories, regions, cities with federal status, autonomous regions and autonomous districts, which are constituent territories of the Russian Federation with equal rights.

The federal form of government of the Russian Federation is based on its national entirety, the uniformity of the system of state authority, the demarcation of competence and powers between the state authorities of the Russian Federation and state authorities of constituent territories of the Russian Federation, equal rights and self-determination of the peoples of the Russian Federation.

The system of state authority in constituent territories of the Russian Federation is governed by the general principles established by the Federation. Each region has a legislative (representative) body (parliament, legislative assembly) and an executive body (government). In many of them there is also a post of Chief Executive Officer (President, Governor). These officers are vested with powers of the legislative authority of the RF constituent territory on the recommendation of the RF President and may hold their positions for an unlimited number of terms.
Russia is also divided into 9 federal districts, each of which has an authorized representative of the RF President.

Constituent territories of the Federation also have administrative territorial divisions. The main units within a constituent territory are municipal and urban districts.

Foreign Policy

Russia is the successor of the USSR in respect of membership of the UN (including the status of a permanent member of the Security Council) and other international organizations, and in participation in international agreements of the USSR. Russia undertook the servicing of the foreign debt of the former USSR. Soviet assets abroad were transferred to Russia.

Russia is one the key members of the international community. As one of the five permanent members of the UN Security Council it remains one of the great powers and bears special responsibility for the maintenance of international peace and security. Russia is a member of the G8 group of economically developed countries, and of a significant number of international organizations, including the Council of Europe and the Organization for Security and Cooperation in Europe. A specific role is played by organizations established on the territory of the former USSR (mainly led by Russia): the Commonwealth of Independent States (CIS), the Eurasian Economic Community (EurAsEC), the Collective Security Treaty Organization (CSTO) and the Shanghai Cooperation Organization (SCO).

Since 1997 Russia and Belarus have formed an Allied State, proposing a political project for an alliance between the Russian Federation and the Republic of Belarus with a common political, economical, military, customs, currency, legal, humanitarian and cultural area organized in stages.

Russian foreign policy is determined by the President and implemented by the Ministry of Foreign Affairs. Russia conducts multi-vector foreign policy. It maintains diplomatic relations with 191 countries and has diplomatic missions in 144 countries.

Investment Policy

Russia supports investment by means of legal, economic and administrative mechanisms. Federal Law No. 160-FZ "On Foreign Investments in the Russian Federation" of 9 July 1999 determines state functions as they relate to the development of the bases and implementation of state policy relating to direct foreign investment, the attraction of direct foreign investment, and Russia's observance of obligations resulting from international agreements.

Foreign capital attracted into the national economy and used effectively, on the one hand, has a positive influence on economic growth and assists Russia's integration into the world economy. The absence of substantial competition on the part of Russian business entities, cheap labor, an extensive market of inexpensive raw materials and an active consumer market make the Russian economy attractive to foreign businessmen.

In 1999, in order to activate investment demand and the more effective use of state investment resources, the Open Joint-Stock Company "Russian Bank for Development" (the Russian state investment bank, now called Joint-Stock Company "Russian Bank for Small and Medium Enterprises Support") and investment guarantee and insurance agencies were established in Russia.

Current investment policy in the Russian Federation is implemented by a number of governmental institutions and organizations:

- The RF Ministry for Economic Development and Trade, whose main function is to participate in the formation of state investment policy.
- The Russian Investment and Tender Corporation, which organizes investment tenders and legal protection of investments. The corporation has a database of Russian and foreign investment bids.

- The State Investment Corporation, created to implement state policy in the investment sphere and to provide foreign investors with political risk guarantees.
- The Russian Financial Corporation, founded with the aim of maintaining effective investment in the country. It is the official agent of the Russian Government for centralized credit management.
- The RF Central Bank, which devises and implements money and credit policy; forms the investment climate in the country; is the agent of the Russian Government for the placement of state loans; establishes a secondary securities market (acts as a broker).

Legal Status of Foreign Nationals

* by Vladimir Kilinkarov, Natalia Zelentsova

In the Russian Federation foreign nationals and stateless persons enjoy the same rights and bear the same responsibilities as citizens of the Russian Federation, unless otherwise determined by federal law or by international treaties to which the Russian Federation is a party. In the Russian Federation persons who are not citizens of Russia and are able to prove that they are citizens of a foreign country shall be considered as foreign nationals. The exercising of rights and liberties by foreign nationals and stateless persons must not infringe the interests of Russian society and the state or the rights and lawful interests of RF citizens and other persons.

Temporary Stay in Russia

In order to enter the Russian Federation a foreign national is required to present a valid identity document recognized as such by the Russian Federation and an entry visa, unless a different procedure of entering the Russian Federation is established by an international treaty. The basis for the issue of a visa or for entry to the Russian Federation without a visa shall be an invitation to enter the Russian Federation. Invitations shall be issued by the Ministry for Foreign Affairs or the Ministry for Internal Affairs or its territorial bodies. Electronic invitation form is available since 27 April, 2015. It is sent by e-mail after submitting all the necessary documents to the federal authority.

The following persons may enter the Russian Federation without a visa:

- citizens of CIS countries and stateless persons permanently residing in those countries who have the right to visa-free entry to Russia;
- persons, whose right to visa-free entry is stipulated by intergovernmental agreements on the terms and procedure for the issuance of visas and agreements on visa-free trips on diplomatic and service passports (crewmembers of foreign airlines whose names of are listed in the agreement; crewmembers of Russian

vessels; foreign tourists on cruises on passenger vessels of both countries during short trips ashore, provided that they do not visit other cities and live on board the vessel). In addition, where an appropriate agreement has been signed, foreign nationals with valid diplomatic and service passports may enter or transit the Russian Federation without obtaining a visa. They may stay in the Russian Federation for 90 days from the date of entry. Employees of diplomatic missions and consular establishments with diplomatic and service passports may stay in the Russian Federation without a visa for the whole period of their official mission. Members of their families with diplomatic or service passports enjoy the same right.

Persons who arrive in the Russian Federation with a visa or who do not require an entry visa, have obtained an immigration card but have no residence permit or temporary residence permit, are considered as foreign nationals **staying temporarily** in the Russian Federation. These persons are obliged to register their foreign travel passports or other documents in lieu of passports in accordance with the established procedure and to leave the Russian Federation on the expiry of the permitted term. The period of temporary stay for a foreign national in the Russian Federation shall be limited by the validity period of the visa granted to that foreign national.

Immigration Registration

The Russian Federation is the second country in the world in terms of the number of immigrants. Immigration, including its statutory regulation, is a complex national problem that requires all factors influencing the situation to be taken into account.

According to the Conception of State Migration Policy of the Russian Federation for the period up to 2025 approved by the President of the RF among the priority goals are the arrangement conditions and incentives for the resettlement in the Russian Federation for permanent residence of fellow-nationals residing abroad, immigrants and certain categories of foreign nationals; development of differentiated mechanisms for selecting and employing foreign labor; the encouragement of internal migration; assisting educational migration and supporting academic mobility; meeting humanitarian commitments in respect of forced migrants; assistance of adaptation and integration of migrants, the formation of constructive interaction between migrants and the host community; resistance of illegal migration.

Immigration legislation in the Russian Federation is constantly developing. In January 2007 a registration requirement for newly arrived immigrants was introduced and the administrative liability of employers using the labor of illegal employees was reinforced. These measures have facilitated the achievement of the goal of obtaining objective information on the immigration situation in the country. The number of immigrants has also increased.

At the same time, Federal Law No. 109-FZ "On the Immigration Registration of Foreign Nationals and Stateless Persons" of 18 July 2006 establishes a fairly complicated mechanism for the immigration registration of a foreign national by place of residence, the registration of a foreign national at the place of his/her stay, and the recording of other information required by law.

Any breach of the immigration registration rules shall be precluded by the immigration authorities – in particular, by the territorial bodies of the Federal Migration Service of the Russian Federation. Any breach of the immigration registration rules may entail administrative liability for both the host party and the foreign national in the form of a fine, and in certain cases may result in the exclusion of the foreign national from the Russian Federation. A foreign national subject to administrative exclusion may be prohibited from entering the Russian Federation for a period of up to five years. The amounts of fines payable within the framework of administrative liability for a breach of the immigration registration rules, together with the complexity and onerousness of such rules for legal entities and individuals, is one of the most significant problems of Russian immigration policy.

The **immigration registration** procedure consists of notifying a territorial body of the Federal Migration Service of the arrival of a foreign national at a place of stay; it must be carried out within seven working days of the arrival of the foreign national in the Russian Federation. In this regard, it is necessary to note that all the procedures relating to immigration registration must be undertaken by the host party. A foreign national is not required to waste time applying to any bodies. On arrival at his/her place of stay, a foreign national shall present his/her passport and the immigration card he/she completed on entering the Russian Federation to the host party.

The following persons may act as host parties: citizens of Russia, foreign nationals and stateless persons permanently residing in Russia (with a residence permit), legal entities, their branches or representative offices where a foreign national actually resides (stays) or works, hotel administration. (when a foreign national stays in a hotel), which are to notify a territorial body of the Federal Migration Service of the arrival of a foreign national within 24 hours, undertake all the necessary procedures relating to the registration of foreign nationals and bear responsibility for their compliance with the established rules of stay. A foreign national may act as a host party in respect of members of his/her family provided that such foreign national is a highly qualified professional and owns residential premises in the Russian Federation (regardless of whether such foreign national has obtained the status of a permanent resident of the Russian Federation or not and irrespective of the area of his/her residential premises).

A foreign national has the right to independently notify the immigration registration authorities of his/her arrival at a place of stay, provided that he/she files documentary evidence of valid reasons (illness, physical impossibility *etc.*) that prevent the host party from notifying the authorities.

Temporary and Permanent Residence in Russia

A temporary residence permit may be granted to a foreign national within the quota established by the Government of the Russian Federation. The demographic situation in the relevant constituent territory of the Russian Federation and the ability of that constituent territory to accept foreign nationals for settlement is taken into account. The validity period of a temporary residence permit is three years. A temporary residence permit may be granted to a foreign national outside the quota established by the Government of the Russian Federation only in exceptional circumstances expressly set out in law (in particular, to a person investing in the Russian Federation the amount established by the RF Government; a person who is married to a Russian citizen; a person with a place of residence in Russia; a person who has a child who is a Russian citizen *etc.*).

Within the validity term of a temporary residence permit, and provided that a foreign national has legal grounds, he/she may apply for and be issued with a **residence permit**. An application for a residence permit shall be submitted by a foreign national to a territorial body of the Federal Migration Service within six months of the expiry of the validity of his/her temporary residence permit. In order to obtain a residence permit a foreign national must have resided in Russia for at least one year on the basis of a temporary residence permit. Highly qualified specialists and their family members as well as foreign nationals recognized native Russian speakers in accordance with federal law may obtain a residence permit under the simplified procedure. A residence permit shall be granted to a foreign national for a period not exceeding 5 years. The residence permit term can be extended an unlimited number of times

A foreign national who holds a Russian residence permit may leave the country using a valid identity document recognized as such by the Russian Federation and the residence permit.

As a general rule, a foreign national when obtaining a temporary residence permit, a residence permit shall confirm his/her Russian language skills, knowledge on Russian history and basic legislative principles.

The Russian Federation grants **political asylum** to foreign nationals and stateless persons in accordance with generally recognized international legal regulations.

Employment

Participation of foreign nationals in labor relations is governed by Federal Law "On Legal Status of Foreign Nationals in the Russian Federation" No. 115-FZ of 25 July 2002. Foreign nationals may freely manage their capacity for work, choose their occupation or profession and exercise the right to exert their abilities and use property for entrepreneurial or other activity permitted by law, subject to the restrictions stipulated by the Federal Law.

A foreign national or a stateless person may be **employed** in Russia upon the obtaining of a work permit if he/she is over 18. In addition, an employer must have permission to invite and engage foreign employees. It should be noted that specific requirements regulating the involvement of foreign nationals in labor relations also cover customers of works (services) engaging foreign employees based on civil law agreements on the performance of work (rendering services).

The specified procedure does not cover, in particular, the following foreign nationals: those permanently or temporary residing in the Russian Federation; those employed by foreign legal entities (manufacturers or suppliers) that perform assembling, support service and warranty maintenance as well as post-warranty repair of technical equipment shipped to the Russian Federation; journalists accredited in the Russian Federation; those invited to the Russian Federation as scientists or teachers, provided that they are invited to carry our research or pedagogic activity by educational organizations of higher education, state academies of sciences or other scientific or innovation organizations; those invited to the Russian Federation for business or humanitarian purposes or in order to be employed and engaged, in addition, in teaching in scientific organizations and educational organizations of higher education; employees of representative offices of foreign legal entities.

An employer and customer of works (services) shall be entitled to attract and engage foreign employees without the respective permission, provided that the foreign employees arrived in the Russian Federation in compliance with a procedure that does not require a visa, they are highly qualified professionals or family members of a highly qualified professional (a foreign national shall be deemed a highly qualified professional if he/she has experience, skills or achievements in a specific field, provided that the terms and conditions of his/her employment in the Russian Federation stipulate that he/she receives salary (remuneration) in the amount set out by law); or they are studying in the Russian Federation on a full-time basis in the professional educational organization or educational organization of higher education or in some other cases.

As a general rule, a foreign national when obtaining a work permit shall also confirm his/her Russian language skills, knowledge on Russian history and basic legislative principles.

An application by a foreign national for a work permit may not be refused, with the exception of cases where the foreign national fails to submit the necessary documents.

A foreign national temporarily arriving or temporarily residing in the Russian Federation may not be employed outside the constituent territory of the Russian Federation where a work permit was issued to him/her.

For more detail on these and other matters relating to employment in Russia, see the *Employment* section of this brochure.

Setting up a New Business

* by Vladimir Kilinkarov, Natalia Zelentsova

In this section we would like to focus your attention on information concerning the basic legal aspects of business organization in Russia, establishing branches and representative offices of foreign companies on its territory and setting up new companies (organizations/legal entities).

You may find general information about acquiring an existing company or organization in Russia in the *Acquisition of a Business* and *Joint Ventures* sections.

We also recommend you to refer to the following sections of this brochure:

* Real Estate & Construction – issues relating to the acquisition of real estate;
* Employment – issues relating to the employment and dismissal of personnel and the regulation of labor activity in a company;
* Taxation – issues relating to taxation of a company's activity;
* Intellectual Property – issues relating to a company's means of individualization (company names, trademarks, commercial symbols).

Legal Forms

Under the civil legislation of the Russian Federation there are two main possibilities for a legally capable person who wishes to engage in business: either to conduct business without forming a legal entity (unincorporated) after registration as an **individual entrepreneur**, or to incorporate a **company** in a legal form determined by law (partnership or company, production or consumer cooperative, institution, fund, *etc.*).

A new business in Russia shall be set up in accordance with the applicable civil legislation, the federal laws on the legal forms of entities that carry out entrepreneurial activity, federal laws on nonprofit-making organizations and other regulations relating to some aspects of the incorporation and operation of organizations.

In setting up a new company it is necessary to choose its legal form in compliance with the RF Civil Code.

Individual Enterprises

The simplest way of organizing a business is to become an **individual entrepreneur**. In accordance with Article 23 of the RF Civil Code a citizen may carry out entrepreneurial activity without establishing a legal entity. He/she starts to enjoy this right from the moment of his/her state registration as an individual entrepreneur. Entrepreneurial activity carried out without forming a legal entity shall be governed by rules set out in the RF Civil Code for legal entities acting as business organizations, unless otherwise stated by other legislative acts.

The advantages of individual enterprises are:

* a simple registration (liquidation) procedure,;
* a simplified procedure for income and expense accounting, no obligation to maintain accounts;
* favorable tax rates.

The main disadvantage of an individual entrepreneur is, above all, the level of responsibility: an individual entrepreneur who does not form a legal entity is liable for his/her obligations by all his/her property. In addition, an individual entrepreneur may not obtain licenses to some licensable types of activity (for example, the retail of some kinds of pharmaceuticals, alcoholic products). Individual enterprises are not suitable for conducting joint business.

Nevertheless, at the initial stage of setting up a business an individual enterprise is often the most suitable form of business. In the event of success, an individual entrepreneur gains the necessary experience and capital required to enter the corporate business category with the formation of a legal entity.

A foreign national or organization may enter the Russian market in various forms, including various types of franchising, dealer, distribution and agency agreements. However, conducting a full-scale business in one's own name while preserving maximum control over the business is possible only in the event of setting up a daughter company or the branch/representative office of a foreign company in Russia.

Branches and Representative Offices of Foreign Organizations

A possible form of business in Russia is the establishment by a foreign company of economically autonomous subdivisions (branches and representative offices).

The provisions of the RF Civil Code regulating business also apply to foreign nationals and legal entities; therefore foreign companies acting in Russia in the form of a branch or representative office enjoy the national regime, i.e. they have the same rights and obligations as Russian organizations, except in cases expressly stipulated by law.

For information about the legal status of branches and representative offices in the Russian Federation and the differentiation of these concepts, see the information below.

In order to establish a branch or a representative office of a foreign organization in Russia it is necessary to go through an accreditation procedure and obtain a special permit. This procedure is governed by Decree of the Council of Ministers of the USSR "On Approval of Regulation on the Procedure of Establishing and Operation of Foreign Representative Offices, Banks and Organizations in the USSR" No. 1074 of 30 November 1989 and the Order of the Central Bank of Russia No. 02-437 of 7 October, 1997 "On procedure of opening and operation of representative offices of foreign credit institutions in the Russian Federation " regarding opening of a representative offices of foreign credit institutions.

In most cases the accreditation of branches and representatives offices of foreign companies in Russia since 2015 is carried out by the Federal Tax Service.

A branch or representative office of a foreign organization shall be deemed established as of the date when the permission to establish such branch or representative office was issued. Subsequently, the branch or representative office may be registered with the tax authorities, open a bank account and start its operations.

Accreditation of employees to a branch or a representative office of a foreign organization shall be carried out by the accreditation body that issued the permission to establish the representative office within the permitted number of employees.

An undoubted advantage for a foreign organization carrying out business through a branch is the availability of various benefits (benefits for renting premises, various customs benefits for specific types of commodities in the course of their transfer across the Russian border). Such benefits is also applied to representative offices from 1 January 2015, according to the recent amendments to the Federal Law «On Foreign Investments in the Russian Federation».

A permit for opening a branch / representative office is issued without any validity period limitations.

One more advantage to be mentioned is that unlike a legal entity, its economically autonomous subdivisions (branches and representative offices) exercise a simplified maintenance of accounts. On the other hand, branches and representative offices do not enjoy the rights of a legal entity and the foreign legal entity is responsible for their activity. In many cases this results in the rejection of this course in favor of the creation of a new company.

Legal Forms of Legal Entities

When choosing a legal form for a legal entity one should be guided by the line and scope of the proposed business, the number of participants (co-founders) and the specific character of the market activity of the future enterprise. Legal entities can only be created in one of the legal forms provided for by the RF Civil Code. In accordance with the RF Civil Code, all legal entities shall be divided into two types: profit-making organizations and nonprofit-making organizations.

Profit-making organizations are legal entities whose main purpose is the generation of profits and their distribution among its participants. Such organizations may be established in the following legal forms: business partnerships, business entities, economic partnerships, peasant (farm) holdings, production co-operatives as well as state and municipal unitary enterprises.

Nonprofit-making organizations may be established only in the forms directly named in the RF Civil Code (in forms of consumer cooperatives, social organizations, associations (unions) including nonprofit-making partnerships, self-regulating organizations, chambers for commerce and industry, chambers of notaries and advocates, real estate owners associations, Cossack societies, the RF native minorities communities, funds institutions, autonomous nonprofit-making organizations, religious organizations and public companies).

The second classification of legal entities stipulated by the RF Civil Code divides them into **corporate legal entities** (corporations), which founders (participants) have the «right of participation (membership)», and **unitary entities**, which founders (participants) have no such right and do not become their members. For corporate and unitary entities the RF Civil Code provides for different special rules on management as well as exercising the rights of participants, etc.

Profit-making corporate organizations whose charter (share) capital is divided into shares (contributions) of their founders are deemed to be business partnerships and business entities. Charter (share) capital means the part of a company's capital intended to guarantee the rights of creditors. The size of the charter (share) capital shall be specified in the company's charter. Charter (share) capital and property acquired in the course of activity is owned by the business partnership or business entity.

Business partnerships may be established in the form of a general partnership or a special partnership (limited partnership). The activity of partnerships is regulated by Part I of the RF Civil Code.

Business partnerships as a form of legal entities should be distinguished from simple partnerships, including investment partnerships that conduct their activity on the basis of a simple partnership agreement (joint activity agreement) without forming an autonomous company.

Business entities may be founded in the form of joint stock companies or companies with limited liability.

The activity of these entities is governed by Part I of the RF Civil Code, Federal Law No. 208-FZ "On Joint Stock Companies" of 26 December 26 1995, and Federal Law No. 14-FZ "On Limited Liability Companies" of 8 February 1998.

Business Partnerships

A **partnership** is deemed **general** if its participants (partners) conduct business activity on behalf of the partnership in accordance with an agreement entered into between them and bear liability for the obligations of the partnership by the property they own.

This form of carrying out business is quite rare. A general partnership is established and acts on the basis of a foundation agreement signed by all its participants. Its activity is managed by the mutual agreement of all the participants. Each participant may act on behalf of the partnership, unless otherwise specified in the agreement. The agreement shall contain provisions relating to the size and composition of share capital; the amount of the share capital belonging to each partner; the size, composition, term and procedure for contribution by the partners; liability for breach of the obligation to make a contribution.

In a **limited partnership (special partnership)**, along with the participants conducting business on behalf of the partnership and bearing liability for the obligations of the partnership by their property, there are one or more limited partners (participants) who bear the risk of losses associated with the activity of the partnership within the limits of their contributions and do not participate in the business activity of the partnership.

Only individual entrepreneurs and profit-making organizations may be participants of general partnerships and general partners in special partnerships. In addition, general partners are jointly liable by their property for the obligations of the partnership.

The foundation agreement executed by any and all general partners shall be the foundation document of a special partnership.

A participant withdrawing from the partnership is liable for obligations of the partnership that arose prior to his/her withdrawal on an equal basis with the remaining participants within two years from the date of approval of the report on the activity of the partnership for the year in which he/she withdrew from the partnership. The said scope of responsibility places a risk for the unsuccessful acts of any participant on each of them. Since general partners bear unlimited liability for the obligations of the partnership and such partnerships are much more attractive for creditors than for the partners thereof. In addition, the specific form of management of the partnership stipulated by law may slow down the decision-making process. These circumstances constitute the basic disadvantages of carrying out business in the form of a partnership.

Business Entities

The most widespread form for the organization of small and medium businesses in Russia is a **limited liability company** (LLC). A limited liability company is a business entity incorporated by one or more persons whose charter capital is divided into interests; the size of the charter capital shall be specified in the foundation documents.

The company's participants (their number may not exceed 50) are not liable for the obligations of the company and bear risk of losses associated with the company's activity within the limit of the value of their contributions. An LLC is the most suitable form for small and medium businesses and the minimum size of its charter capital is not great (10,000 rubles). Information relating to the members of an LLC is reflected in the Unified State Register of Legal Entities. A change in participants requires registration in the said register. Unlike other legal entities, an LLC may consist of one person (individual). If an entrepreneur becomes the sole participant and the general director, he/she may totally control his/her business. At the same time, in order to protect interests of the creditors of such LLC, the RF Civil Code Draft Amendments directly provide for the subsidiary liability of the sole participant the LLC for obligations which arise as the result of fulfilling the instructions of the sole participant.

The foundation document of an LLC is its charter.

The supreme management body of an LLC is a general meeting of its participants. Day-to-day management is conducted by the sole executive body (president, general director, *etc.*). Charter of LLC as well as foundation documents of other types of corporations may provide several persons acting jointly execute the powers of the sole executive body, or may contain provisions about several sole executive bodies acting independently. A board of directors and a collegial management body (directorate, management board, *etc.*) may be established if required. A company's charter may provide for the establishment of an internal audit commission (election of internal auditor) of a company. It is mandatory to establish an internal audit commission (elect an internal auditor) for companies with more than fifteen participants. An independent auditor may act as an internal auditor.

The size of a participant's interests is the ratio between the nominal value of such interests and the size of the charter capital. The number of votes of each participant of the company at the general meeting is equal to the size of his/her interests in the charter capital. The actual value of the interest of each participant of an LLC corresponds to the portion of the company's assets pro rata the size of his/her interest.

The company itself may not acquire interests in its charter capital, except in cases expressly stipulated by law. A participant of a company shall be entitled to sell or otherwise alienate his/her interest in the charter capital of an LLC or part thereof in favor of one or several participants of the company. The consent of other participants of the company or the company itself is not required, unless otherwise specified in the company's charter. The sale or other alienation of interest or part thereof in favor of third persons is permitted, unless prohibited by the company's charter. However, other participants of the company enjoy a preemption right to the purchase of the said interest or part thereof. A transaction purposed to alienate interest in the charter capital of the company or part thereof is subject to notarization. Failure to observe this notarization requirement will render the transaction invalid.

An LLC participant may withdraw from the company if it is provided for by the charter or by way of claiming LLC to purchase interest in the cases provided by law. From the moment of the submission by a participant of an application to withdraw, his/her interest shall be transferred to the company, which is obliged to pay the actual value of such interest to the participant.

A company may distribute profits between its participants on a quarterly, half-yearly or annual basis.

One of the disadvantages of LLCs is that they are unattractive for creditors, as LLC participants bear restricted liability for the obligations of the LLC within the value of the participatory interests that belong to them.

As a general rule a participant of a business entity is not liable for the entity's obligations and bears the risks of losses incurred as a result of the entity's activity within the value of the participatory interests (shares) belonging to him/her. However, the law may provide otherwise. For example, the provisions of the Federal Law "On Insolvency (Bankruptcy)" No. 127-FZ of 26 October 2002 (see Bankruptcy Law below) stipulate cases when participants and a director of a business entity shall bear subsidiary liability for the obligations of such business entity. in the event of:

1) bankruptcy of the business entity through the fault of its participants (shareholders) or other persons entitled to give instructions that are binding upon the business entity or such persons that otherwise may govern its actions; if a business entity participant did not pay for his/her shares (participatory interests in the charter capital) in such entity in full - within the value of the unpaid part of his/her shares (participatory interests in the charter capital) in such business entity;

2) transformation of a partnership into a company - within two years for the obligations transferred to the company from the partnership.

The provisions of the Insolvency Law stipulate other events when subsidiary liability for the obligations of the obliged company is imposed on the persons who breached the provisions of the law (for example, on the head of the company if accounting documents and/or accounts are unavailable or contain no such information on the assets and obligations of the obligor and their flow that is to be collected, registered and crystallized on a mandatory basis).

A **joint-stock company** (JSC) is a profit-making organization whose charter capital is divided into a specific number of shares. Shareholders are not liable for the obligations of the company and bear risk associated with the company's activity within the limits of the value of their shares.

Joint-stock companies are divided into **public** and **nonpublic** ones. Securities of a public joint-stock company are publicly placed (by means of public offering) or publicly listed subject to the terms and conditions set out by the securities laws. Other joint-stock companies are recognized non-public.

The Civil Code provides a number of special rules in relation to public joint stock companies.

A public joint-stock company is required to submit information on its name, containing an indication that the company is public, for inclusion in the Unified State Register of Legal Entities. From the moment of inclusion of this information in the said register a JSC acquires the right to place shares publicly. In a public joint-stock company a collective management body is formed from not less than five members. An independent organization with the appropriate license is responsible for maintaining the register of shareholders and performance of the functions of the Counting Commission in a public joint-stock company. The number of shares held by one shareholder, their total nominal value and the maximum number of votes granted to one shareholder cannot be limited in a public joint-stock company. The necessity to obtain someone's consent for alienation of shares also cannot be provided for by the charter of a public joint-stock company. As a general rule, no one may be granted the right of preferential purchase of shares of a public joint-stock company.

These joint stock companies may be subject to special legal regulation and additional requirements ensuring a greater degree of transparency and publicity in the company's management and reporting as compared to nonpublic joint-stock companies.

A public joint-stock company is a promising form for a major business. It makes it possible for shareholders to dispose of their shares freely. Within the framework of the activity of this legal form of organization the interests of the owners are met, additional capital may be raised by means of the issuance of shares.

In connection with the amendment of the civil legislation the general provisions regulating joint stock companies were changed materially. For example, joint stock companies are no longer divided into open and closed companies.

Please find below a comparative analysis of such legal forms as LLC, JSC and Economic Partnerships in compliance with the RF corporate law as of 01 May 2015.

	LLC	JSC	Economic Partnerships
Maximum number of participants	50	Not restricted	50. A partnership management agreement may restrict the total number of participants.
Foundation documents	Charter	Charter, where it is required to register issuance of shares upon incorporation of a company	Charter
Minimum size of charter capital	10,000 rubles	100,000 rubles	—
Property contributed as a contribution to the charter capital	Monies, items, shares in charter (share) capital of other business entities and partnerships, state and municipal bonds. The exclusive and other intellectual rights and right under the license agreements subject to monetary valuation can also be such a contribution. The company charter or law may impose restrictions. At the moment of paying charter capital a contribution not less than the minimal amount of charter capital shall be made by monies. The monetary evaluation of in-kind contributions to charter capital shall be made by an independent appraiser. The company participants are not allowed to male decision on monetary value of in-kind contributions in amount exceeding estimates, determined by an independent appraiser.		Monies, items or other property interests or other rights having monetary value. Securities may not be contributed to the share capital, with the exception of the business entities' bonds determined by the authorized executive authority in the area of the financial markets. The partnership management agreement may set out other restrictions. Unless otherwise provided by the partnership management agreement, the monetary value of property and other objects of the civil law rights contributed into the share capital shall be approved by the unanimous decision of all the partners. In the event of failure to reach a decision on the monetary value or on the assessment of the appraiser, the contribution shall be made in monetary form.

	LLC	JSC	Economic Partnerships
Increasing in the charter capital	Amendments to the foundation documents must be registered	Amendments to the foundation documents must be registered; issuance of shares must be registered; an issuance statement must be registered.	Amendments to the foundation documents must be registered
Confidentiality of participants	Medium. Information on the participants is contained in the list of participants (maintained by the company) and in the Unified State Register of Legal Entities (EGRUL)	Comparatively high. Information on the shareholders is contained only in the shareholders register (maintained by the company or by a special registrar, who provides information only upon the request of state bodies). Information on the initial shareholders (founders) is contained in the Unified State Register of Legal Entities (EGRUL)	Medium. Information on the shareholders is contained in the Unified State Register of Legal Entities (EGRUL) and the register of partners (to be maintained by the partnership)
Change of participants	Subject to registration of changes in EGRUL without amendment of the charter	Reflected only in the shareholders register	Information on the partners is subject to registration in EGRUL without amendment of the charter

	LLC	JSC	Economic Partnerships
Right to purchase interests and shares + consent	Participants have a preemptive right to the purchase of interests in the event of their alienation in favor of third persons. The charter may provide for the preemptive right to the purchase of interest by the company if the other participants of the company did not exercise their preemptive right. The participant of a company shall not require the prior consent of other participants of the company or the company itself to alienate his/her interests, unless otherwise stipulated in the company's charter. A participatory interest may be alienated in favor of third persons, unless prohibited by the company charter.	Shareholders may freely alienate their shares in favor of third persons without prior offer to other shareholders as well as without their prior consent	Unless otherwise provided by the partnership management agreement, a partner shall be entitled to alienate his/her share in share capital in favor of another partner, the partnership or a third party. The partners and the partnership shall enjoy the preemptive right to purchase a share in the share capital over the rights of third parties, unless otherwise stipulated in the partnership management agreement. The partnership management agreement may provide for various procedures regulating obtaining consent of the partners to the transfer of a share in the share capital to third parties depending on such transfer or other circumstances.

	LLC	JSC	Economic Partnerships
Withdrawing from a company	A participant may withdraw from a company at any time if it is provided for in the company's charter. The actual price for his/her interest shall be paid to the participant or the participant shall be given property whose value corresponds to such price in kind. (The participant is entitled to withdraw from the company regardless whether or not the other participants of the company or the company itself give their/its consent).	Withdrawal is possible only by means of the sale of shares without right to the company's assets. The company may buy out shares only in a limited number of cases	As a general rule the partners are prohibited from withdrawing from the partnership, unless otherwise stipulated in the partnership management agreement.
Management structure	As a rule it consists of two levels: a general meeting of the participants and an executive body (either collegial or sole)	As a rule it consists of three levels: a general meeting of shareholders, a board of directors and an executive body, but it is possible to transfer the authority of the board of directors to another commercial organization or individual entrepreneur (upon a decision of the general meeting).	The system, structure, and scope of authority of the management bodies of the company, the procedure for conducting activity and termination thereof shall be set out in the partnership management agreement. However, the partnership may not operate without a properly elected sole executive body.
Interest (share) pledge	A decision on a pledge of interest of a participant in favor of another participant or, unless prohibited by the charter, to a third party, shall be made by a general meeting of the participants	A shareholder does not require the consent of the company for a share pledge	A partner is not entitled to pledge his/her share in the share capital of the partnership.

	LLC	JSC	Economic Partnerships
Decisions of general meetings	Decisions by a general meeting of participants shall be made by the proportion of the total number of votes determined by law or in the charter (each participant has a number of votes proportionate to his/her contribution to the charter capital). There is no concept of a quorum.	Decisions by a general meeting of shareholders shall be made by the proportion of the total number of votes determined by law or in the charter (1 vote equals 1 share). The concept of a quorum applies. In a public JSC the maximum number of votes granted to one shareholder cannot be restricted.	The procedure for decision making shall be determined in the partnership management agreement. On issues related to the amendment of the partnership management agreement each partner thereto shall have one vote, regardless of the size of his/her share in the share capital of the partnership.
Requirement of unanimous decisions of the general meeting	Resolutions on matters relating to restructuring or liquidation and certain other issues shall be adopted unanimously at the general meeting of participants.	No matters requiring unanimous decisions fall within the authority of the general meeting of shareholders, with the exception of the company's transformation into a nonprofit partnership.	Acceptance of new partners, exclusion of some partners, approval of the monetary value of objects of the civil law rights contributed to the share capital, election of the sole executive body, reorganization in the form of transformation, etc.
Authority of management bodies	The charter may invest the board of directors with greater powers than those granted by law.		The powers of the management bodies of the partnership are set out in the partnership management agreement. The obligations of the sole executive body are determined by law.
Restriction of transactions	There are statutory limits for major transactions and related party transactions that can be made by director. It is also possible to impose additional restrictions by the general meeting of shareholders and the board of directors (if any) to those and other transactions by director.		The nature and the scope of authorities of the sole executive body and other management bodies of the partnership relating to the conducting and/or approval of some or other steps or transactions is regulated by the partnership management agreement.

	LLC	JSC	Economic Partnerships
Possibility of excluding a participant	By a court decision in certain circumstances (for example, if actions (or inaction) of a participant has caused substantial damage to the company, etc.)		A partner can be excluded by a court decision if a partner fails to observe his/ her obligation to make a contribution into the share capital, subject to the unanimous decision of all the other partners.
Possibility of levying execution on interests (shares)	By a court decision, only in the event that no other property is available.	Mainly by a court decision or after levying execution on liquid property.	Permitted only by a court decision if the partner's property is insufficient to repay the debts.

Corporate agreement

All or some of the participants / shareholders of a business entity may enter into an agreement on the exercising of their corporate rights also called «rights of membership» (corporate agreement), under which they undertake to exercise their rights and/or refrain from exercising such rights in a specified manner, including voting in a certain way at the general meeting of the participants of the company, agreeing a form of voting with other participants (shareholders), selling an interest or part thereof (acquiring or alienating shares) at a price determined in such an agreement and/or under certain circumstances refraining from the alienation of interest (share) or a part thereof until certain circumstances occur.

Such an agreement shall be executed in writing by means of drawing up a single document to be signed by the parties thereto.

Economic Partnership

From 1 July 2012 in the Russian Federation it will be permitted to form an economic partnership, a new type of profit-making organization (See Federal Law "On Economic Partnerships" No. 380-FZ of 3 December 2011).

An economic partnership may be established by two or more members. However, the number of members may not exceed fifty. Both individuals and legal entities may become members of the partnership.

However, it is not only prohibited for a sole member to form such a partnership, but also the situation when after the formation of such a partnership only one member remains in it is impermissible (in this event the mandatory liquidation or reorganization of the partnership is provided for).

As a general rule, the partners are prohibited to withdraw from the partnership unless otherwise provided for in the partnership management agreement. New members may be accepted into the partnership only subject to the consent of all other members. The preemptive right to purchase a share in the share capital is also provided for. Moreover, as a general rule the preemptive right is established not only for the members, but for the partnership also. It is also prohibited to pledge a share in the partnership. If this prohibition is lifted in the partnership management agreement, the pledge is permitted only subject to the consent of all other members.

The law sets out the general legal capacity for economic partnerships. However, it imposes certain restrictions in respect of the operations of a partnership (for example, an economic partnership may not issue bonds and other equity securities, advertise its activity, establish legal entities or participate in them, except for unions and associations). However, the existence of these restrictions may not be regarded as establishing a special legal capacity for economic partnerships.

The foundation document of an economic partnership is its charter. The charter shall specify not only the partnership's objective, but also the specific activities that partnership may engage in.

The law on economic partnerships does not indicate that other provisions not contradicting the legislation may be included in the charter. This provision serves as the grounds for interpreting the list of provisions of the charter of an economic partnership as exhaustive. There are therefore a number of provisions which, although usually included in a charter, may not be added to the charter of an economic entity: for example, a provision prohibiting the director to consummate interested-party transactions.

In addition to the charter the partnership management agreement plays a significant role in regulating the operations of an economic partnership. Specifically, it sets out both the scope and nature of the authority of the sole executive body and other management bodies of the partnership relating to the conducting and/or approval of specific steps or transactions. For instance, the agreement may restrict the scope of authorities of the executive bodies. However, the partnership agreement is an internal document and, as a general rule, third parties are not aware of the content thereof. Therefore, the partnership, the partners to the partnership and other members to the partnership management agreement may not refer to its provisions in their relations with third parties. An exception is the situation where the said persons can prove that a third party knew or should have known about the content of the agreement when a transaction was conducted.

The minimum size of the charter capital of an economic partnership is not determined. Therefore, its charter capital may equal one ruble.

Legislators have introduced specific measures for the protection of partnership property that are not established for other legal forms. Rights to the results of intellectual activity owned by the partnership shall be specially protected.

When it is required to levy execution on intellectual property rights (for more details please see the *Intellectual Property* section) in order to fulfill the partnership's obligations, (a) member(s) of the partnership may independently fulfill the partnership's obligations and contractors are obliged to accept such fulfillment of obligations. This emphasizes that initially an economic partnership is supposed to create additional opportunities for venture investments in IP and IT, although the Law on Economic Partnerships does not restrict the area of application of this legal form.

A rule is also established by law according to which it is possible to levy execution on a partnership member's share in connection with the separate debts of that partnership member only pursuant to a court decision, if the other property of the obliged member is insufficient to repay such indebtedness. Moreover, the member's creditors may not claim for the interest in kind. Only payment of the interest's value by the partnership or its members is permitted.

The principal characteristic of economic partnership management is that only the General Director may act as its sole executive body. It is not permitted to form management boards, boards of directors or other collegial executive bodies. Only an individual who is a member of the partnership may be elected as its General Director. The authority of the General Director is analogous to that of a director of a business entity.

There are certain restrictions on a partnership's activity. For example, a partnership is prohibited from advertising its activity or issuing securities. The partnership is also not permitted to act as the founder of or a participant in other legal entities, except for associations.

Therefore, under the aegis of this legal form one should carry out activity which does not require the promotion or participation of other persons in its charter capital to be successful.

When selecting this legal form one should take into account that it may be transformed into a joint stock company only.

Branches and Representative Offices

Under RF civil legislation a legal entity may open branches and representative offices. A **representative office** is an economically autonomous subdivision of a legal entity situated outside the place of the legal entity's location, which represents and protects the interests of the legal entity. A **branch** is also an economically autonomous subdivision, but it is established in order to perform the functions of the legal entity in whole or in part, including the functions of a representative office. It should be noted that neither representative offices nor branches are legal entities. They are invested with property by the legal entities that establish them and operate on the basis of a power of attorney.

It is obligatory to specify representative offices and branches in the foundation documents of their legal entity.

State Registration

State registration is a necessary stage in the incorporation of legal entities and individual entrepreneurs. It requires a single application by a person to the registration authority, after that the information is to be put to the unified state register and simultaneously tax registration is to be done. On the basis of information in the unified state registers received by bodies of state non-budgetary funds from registration authorities, the registration of legal entities and individual entrepreneurs as insured persons (without direct application to those funds) is carried out.

State registration of the incorporation of a legal entity shall be carried out at the location of such legal entity with the territorial tax authorities, with departments carrying out registration and keeping records on taxpayers, with the exception of some tax inspectorates.

Russian Federation legislation governing state registration includes the Civil Code of the Russian Federation, the Federal Law "On the State Registration of Legal Entities and Individual Entrepreneurs" and other legal acts of the Russian Federation issued in accordance with them. These acts, provides for the registration procedure and the list of grounds for refusal of registration body to register a company.

For the state registration of a legal entity being created the following documents are to be provided:

* an application confirming that the foundation documents submitted comply with the legislative requirements and the information contained therein and in other documents is true and the procedure established for the incorporation of legal entity was duly observed;
* a resolution on establishing a legal entity;
* the foundation documents of a legal entity in two copies;
* an extract from the register of legal entities of the respective country of incorporation or other proof of the legal status of a foreign entity acting as a founder having equal legal force;
* a document confirming payment of state duty.

The registration of an organization or individual entrepreneur with the tax authority at the place of location or place of residence shall be carried out on the basis of information relating to the establishment (including by means of restructuring) of a legal entity, the obtaining by an individual of the status of an individual entrepreneur contained in the relevant record entered in the Unified State Register of Legal Entities and the Unified State Register of Individual Entrepreneurs.

Amendments to the information on organizations or individual entrepreneurs recorded in the register and deregistration in the event of a change of location of a legal entity or place of residence of an individual entrepreneur shall be carried out based on the information reflected in the relevant record in the corresponding state registers.

Tax registration of an organization or individual entrepreneur at a new location or new place of residence shall be carried out based on information received from the tax authority at the previous location or previous place of residence. The date of entry of the respective records in the state registers shall be deemed to be the date of the tax registration of an entity or an individual entrepreneur at a location or place of residence.

In the event of state registration being refused, the decision must contain the grounds of refusal and mandatory reference to specific breaches. A refusal decision shall be delivered to the person specified in the state registration application, with notification of delivery, and may be appealed in court provided it has been previously appealed in pre-judicial order in higher registering body. The law on state registration contains an exhaustive list of grounds for the refusal of state registration. These grounds are as follows: breach of the procedure for the incorporation of a legal entity prescribed by law; non-compliance of the foundation documents of a legal entity with the law; failure to provide documents required for state registration; filing documents with the improper registration authority. Breach of the procedure for the incorporation of a company means, for example, failure to observe the requirements of the procedure for the incorporation of the company (to its participants); of the procedure for making the decision on its incorporation; of the payment of its charter capital, *etc.* provided by law .

Statistical codes shall be assigned by the Federal State Statistics Service of the Russian Federation. Assignment of the statistical codes (OKPO, OKGU, OKATO, OKONH, OKFS, OKOPF) shall be carried out within a few days.

The Social Insurance Fund, the Mandatory Medical Insurance Fund and the Pension Fund are the non-budgetary funds that require mandatory registration of each newly formed legal entity or individual entrepreneur. Upon receiving evidence of the registration of a legal entity or individual entrepreneur, the foregoing funds shall within five working days register the organization and mail the insurance certificate or notification of an insured person. The fund is further obliged to submit the registration number to the relevant tax authority.

Opening of a settlement account. Banking service rules stipulate that one of the conditions for opening a bank account for a newly established company is the availability of its own stamp. The bank first opens an accumulation account, to which at least half the minimum amount of the charter capital shall be credited. As soon as the stamp is available, the bank closes the accumulation account and opens a settlement account to which amounts of contributions of the founders (charter fund) shall be credited. Within a few days (required for the verification of documents) the bank shall enter into a bank account agreement with the firm represented by its director.

A legal entity shall be deemed established from the moment of the entry of the relevant record in the Unified State Register of Legal Entities.

Notification of organizing certain types of entrepreneurial activity

According to Article 8 of Federal Law No. 294-FZ "On the Protection of the Rights of Legal Entities and Individual Entrepreneurs in the Course of Exercising State Control (Supervision) and Municipal Control" of 26 December 2008, individual entrepreneurs and legal entities, when organizing certain types of business activity, shall notify the local branch of the authorized federal executive body, namely the Federal Service for Consumer Rights and Human Welfare Protection, or the Federal Transport Supervision Service, or the Federal Bio-Medical Agency or other authorities specified by law, depending on the types of activity and services.

A legal entity or individual entrepreneur shall notify the authorized federal executive body of the organization of certain types of entrepreneurial activity immediately after state registration and tax registration and prior to the actual commencement of performing works or rendering services.

A legal entity or an individual entrepreneur shall also notify the corresponding body in the event of changing the location and/or place of activity for a legal entity, or the place of residence for an individual entrepreneur, and in the event of the restructuring of a legal entity.

These activity types include hotel services, including short-term accommodation and lodging, retail and wholesale, certain types of transportation services, printing and publishing services, services relating to the use of computers and information technology and the production of certain types of food and non-food products, among others.

The procedure for submitting this and other information is established by RF Government Decree No. 584 of 16 July 2009.

Business location. Special economic zones

Special Economic Zones (SEZs) may be created across the Russian Federation in order to support the development of the manufacturing sector, high technology industries, tourism, health resorts, port infrastructure and transport infrastructure; the development of new technologies and commercialization of outcomes; and the production of new product types.

Depending on the purpose, SEZ types are as follows:

1) industrial/developmental zones;
2) technical/innovational zones;
3) tourist zones;
4) port zones.

For 1 May 2015 there are 17 special economic zones in the Russian Federation, including 6 industrial zones, 5, technical zones, 4 tourist zones and 2 logistics zones.

According to Federal Law No. 116-FZ "On Special Economic Zones in the Russian Federation" of 22 July 2005 (hereinafter, the SEZ Law), a SEZ is a geographical region within the Russian Federation, defined by the Russian Federation Government, wherein special conditions of entrepreneurial activity are established, and the customs procedure applicable to free trade zones may be applied.

Thus, the customs procedure applicable to free trade zones may not be used in tourist and recreational SEZs.

In addition to special conditions of entrepreneurial activity, SEZs are characterized by specific procedures for their creation and management, as well as for overseeing the business activity of its residents.

Special conditions of entrepreneurial activity inside a SEZ include a more favorable environment for entrepreneurial activity, which allows for lower business expenses (according to data provided by Special Economic Zones, by 30 %).

SEZ residents are thus entitled to:

• tax incentives, such as land tax exemption and transport tax exemption;
• preferences, such as incentive rates for the lease of premises and favorable utility connection terms;
• lower administrative burden (the "one-stop" principle);
• infrastructure for developing their own business;
• reduced insurance rates.

For example, the following privileges and preferences are granted to investors of a technical/innovational SEZ in Saint-Petersburg:

- property tax exemption;
- land tax exemption;
- VAT exemption;
- lower insurance rates of 14 %;
- right to the customs procedure applicable to free trade zones;
- incentive rates for the lease of premises;
- favorable terms for connection to the power grid;
- legal safeguards that guarantee privileges and are set out in the Agreement on conducting business activity in a technical/innovational SEZ in Saint-Petersburg.

SEZs are created by the decision of the Russian Federation Government, based on criteria for the creation of a SEZ for forty-nine years.

The SEZ Law sets out a list of activity types that are not permitted within a SEZ. However, the Russian Federation Government may, from time to time, define other activity types. The rules regulating entrepreneurial activity, as well as activity types within a SEZ, vary for different SEZ types.

Infrastructure within a SEZ, including the creation of engineering, transport, social and innovative infrastructure facilities, among others, is funded from the federal budget, budgets of constituent territories of the Russian Federation and local budgets.

Either an individual entrepreneur or a profit-making organization (except for unitary enterprises) may be a resident of a technical/innovational zone or a tourist and recreational zone. Only a profit-making organization (except for unitary enterprises) may be a resident of an industrial/developmental zone or port zone.

Such entities shall be registered in the municipal unit territory within which the special economic zone is created and shall sign an agreement on conducting activities within a SEZ with the authorized federal executive body and a management company. According to this agreement, the management company for instance undertakes obligations to create infrastructure facilities within the zone.

The resident also undertakes various obligations. Thus, a resident of an industrial/developmental zone undertakes to make capital investments of a total of no less that one hundred and twenty million rubles (except for intangible assets), of which no less than forty million rubles (except for intangible assets) shall be invested within three years of the date of the signing of the agreement on conducting business activity.

The resident shall assist the authorities responsible for managing the special economic zone in terms of controlling terms and conditions of the agreement on conducting business activity.

The agreement shall be executed in writing as a single document signed by the parties and concluded for a term not exceeding the remaining term of the special economic zone.

Any amendments to the agreement on conducting business activity shall be executed as a separate agreement thereto.

An individual entrepreneur or a profit-making organization are acknowledged as residents of a special economic zone from the date when a corresponding entry is made in the register of SEZ residents, of which the federal executive body shall notify the corresponding tax and customs authorities, as well as the control authorities for insurance payments.

A resident of a special economic zone ceases to be one only in cases stipulated by law and only subject to judicial procedure.

A resident of a special economic zone may neither establish branches or representative offices outside the special economic zone, nor assign its rights and obligations under the agreement on conducting business activity to any third parties.

The agreement on conducting business activity may be terminated by mutual agreement of the parties or by a party's request in case of a material breach by the other party, material changes in circumstances or on other grounds provided for by the Federal Law.

In the event of the agreement on conducting business activity being terminated, the person shall cease to be a resident of the special economic zone.

Please visit the Special Economic Zones' website: www.russez.ru.

Joint Ventures

* by Vladimir Kilinkarov

The Russian term "joint venture" traditionally encompasses a specific form of business cooperation between a Russian organization or individual with a foreigner, which assumes the formation of joint assets of the partners to be used for the purposes of the functioning of a business. As a rule, a joint venture implies joint corporate participation (joint share holding) of partners in a separate, third organization and joint management by that third party.

It should be noted that the term "joint venture" is not used in Russian legislation. In the Federal Law "On Foreign Investment in the Russian Federation" No. 160-FZ of 9 July 9 1999 the term "commercial organization with foreign investment" is used instead. A Russian commercial organization acquires the status of a commercial organization with foreign investment from the date when a foreign investor joins the organization. As of this date the commercial organization with foreign investment and the foreign investor enjoy legal protection, guarantees and advantages under the said federal law.

Joint ventures are incorporated in Russia in accordance with the same procedure as Russian organizations. Their tax obligations have some specific characteristics, but in general they correspond to the obligations of any other Russian legal entity. As a general rule, the legal regime regulating the activity of foreign investors and the allocation of profit from investments may not be less favorable than the legal regime regulating the activity of Russian investors, with the exceptions provided for by federal laws. It can therefore be said that the regime regulating the activity of foreign investors and joint ventures organized by them in Russia is absolutely the same as the regime regulating the activity of national investors.

Both joint ventures and foreign investors themselves enjoy special guarantees and concessions in Russia, including customs concessions, guarantees of legal protection, provision of proper dispute resolution, availability of various forms of investment, transfer of the rights and obligations of a foreign investor to another person, guarantee of compensation in the event of nationalization and seizure of property, guarantees against an unfavorable (for a foreign investor and a commercial organization with foreign investment) amendment of the relevant Russian legislation, guarantees associated with the allocation in the Russian Federation and transfer from the Russian Federation of profits and other legally earned funds *etc.* (see Articles 15-16 of the aforementioned law).

Among the most common forms of commercial joint ventures in Russia are business entities with joint participation (limited liability companies or joint-stock companies) or ordinary partnerships (a form of joint activity without the incorporation of a legal entity).

The issue of the organization of a joint venture arises when a foreign investor becomes interested in a comprehensive presence on the market of particular goods, works or services where reliable investment is required, as well as comprehensive and effective control over the activities of the object of investment in Russia. In the situation described, simpler mechanisms assuming the conclusion of distribution and dealer agreements between Russian and foreign partners may not fully regulate the investment relations of the parties or provide them with sufficiently wide-ranging guarantees and controlling authority.

It therefore becomes necessary to organize a joint venture, and a proposed investor faces a dilemma relating to the choice of an adequate form for conducting business jointly. The partners have to choose between contract and corporate cooperation models.

The first one, the contract cooperation model, involves the parties entering into a so-called "ordinary partnership agreement" (**"joint activity agreement"**). Issues relating to the execution, performance and termination of an ordinary partnership agreement are touched upon in Article 55 of the RF Civil Code. Pursuant to Article 1041 of the RF Civil Code, under an ordinary partnership agreement two or more persons (partners) undertake to combine their contributions and act jointly, without forming a legal entity for the purposes of gaining profit or achieving any other goal permitted by law.

Funds, other assets, professional or other knowledge, experience, skills, business reputation and business contacts may be contributed.

Assets contributed by the partners of which they had right of ownership, products manufactured as a result of their joint activity, other results of such activity and revenues shall be regarded as their joint shared ownership, unless otherwise established by law or under an ordinary partnership agreement, or result from an essence of obligation. Contributed assets that were owned by the partners on grounds other than property rights shall be used for the benefit of all the partners and constitute the joint property of the partners together with property owned by them jointly.

In the course of conducting joint affairs, each partner may act on behalf of all the partners, unless the ordinary partnership agreement specifies that affairs are to be conducted by certain parties to the ordinary partnership agreement or by all parties thereto jointly. In relations with third parties the authority of a partner to perform transactions on behalf of all the partners shall be confirmed by a power of attorney or by an ordinary partnership agreement executed in writing.

Unlike business entities, where the rights and obligations of the partners are determined not only and not merely by agreements between the partners but by a charter, the amendment procedure for which is understandably quite complicated and formal, requiring not only a discretionary decision of the shareholders but also the registration of such amendments in the Unified State Register of Legal Entities. An ordinary partnership agreement is fairly flexible, though its amendment requires the unanimous agreement of all parties. Unlike the shareholders in a joint-stock company, the parties to an ordinary partnership agreement are entitled to separate the right to manage and the receipt of profits from the size of their contribution. It is determined that decisions relating to the common affairs of the partners shall be made by mutual agreement of the partners, unless otherwise specified in the ordinary partnership agreement. Profits gained by the partners as a result of their joint activity shall be distributed in proportion to the value of their contribution to the joint business, again unless otherwise specified in the ordinary partnership agreement or otherwise agreed by the partners. Any decision prohibiting any of the partners from participating in the distribution of profits shall be null and void.

A specific feature of ordinary partnerships organized in order to conduct business activity jointly is the fact that the partners are jointly liable for all their joint obligations, regardless of how they arise. Each partner is liable for all his/her assets, which naturally does not contribute to the popularity of this form of joint activity.

It is also important to note that, unlike limited liability companies, which do not permit the withdrawal of participants unless otherwise expressly specified in its charter, or joint-stock companies, which permit no withdrawals, an ordinary partnership provides for the possibility of cancelling an ordinary partnership agreement of unspecified duration (with three months prior notification) and the possibility of filing a claim on the termination of such an agreement in court, but only on the basis of a valid excuse and on condition of the recovery of actual damage caused by the termination.

It is therefore advisable to choose the ordinary partnership model, where the partners do not wish to bind themselves by additional formalities related to the registration and maintenance of a Russian legal entity, and where there is no need to be represented in the market as a single company and to incur the expenses associated with it. In addition, an ordinary partnership does not have strict requirements relating to the form of contribution and its evaluation, the procedure of management and the distribution of profits among the partners. Nevertheless, if the activity of the partners involves significant financial risks, an ordinary partnership is less favorable than an LLC or JSC, whose participants (shareholders) are liable for the company's obligations only to the extent of the value of their contribution (shares held by them).

The **corporate cooperation model** requires the establishment of a business partnership or company, the most appropriate and effective legal forms of which are a joint-stock company and a limited liability company. In this case, a foreign investor has another choice to make – whether to invest funds in an existing company and become its rightful participant (shareholder), or to form a new joint venture (by means of incorporation or reorganization, including by means of consolidation or acquisition).

For details of each of the above options please see the respective chapters of this brochure:

* *Setting up a new business* – regarding the specific characteristics of various legal forms of start-ups;
* *Business restructuring* – regarding the specific characteristics of the reorganization of a business by means of consolidation or acquirement with foreign capital involved;
* *Acquisition of a business* – regarding the acquisition of shares and interest in an existing business.

Investment Partnership

On 1 January 2012 Federal Law "On Investment Partnership" No. 335-FZ of 28 November 2011 (hereinafter referred to as the "**Investment Partnership Law**") was enacted in the Russian Federation.

The law aims to create a legal environment for attracting investment into the Russian economy and implementing investment projects based on investment partnership agreements. The lawmakers specified that they "wanted to provide an organizational framework in Russian law that would be analogous to European collective investment schemes".

The Principal Advantages and Restrictions of an Investment Partnership

The investment partnership structure is intended to combine the advantages of business partnerships with those of ordinary partnerships, while eliminating their respective principal disadvantages.

The fundamental principle of the legislative regulation of an investment partnership agreement is the availability in the structure of the agreement of the maximum possible number of options for the participants in the partnership to establish rules convenient to them.

Other advantages of the said contract model are the split of responsibilities between its participants and additional guarantees relating to the consistency of its structure and the composition of its managing partners. Contributions of partners are additionally protected. Another advantage is the fairly long period (up to 15 years).

It should be noted that this form of conducting business is available for investment activity only.

Among other restrictions, you are not permitted to decline participation or transfer your rights if you are not a managing partner. You are not permitted to render your contribution in kind or advertise the partnership activity. The practice of attracting new partners by means of public offer is also restricted.

Particular Features of an Investment Partnership

An investment partnership is a kind of ordinary partnership. General provisions on ordinary partnerships are set out in Article 55 of the Civil Code.

As in an ordinary partnership, an investment partnership constitutes an association of two or more persons for achieving a specific goal, namely for gaining profits. Persons enter into an investment partnership under an investment partnership agreement. In this event no legal entity shall be formed.

The main feature common to both ordinary partnerships and investment partnerships is the availability of common property and common participatory share ownership of partners and the need to separate the common property of the partners.

What distinguishes an investment partnership from an ordinary partnership?

An investment partnership differs from an ordinary partnership principally by the parties to the investment partnership agreement and the activities the partners of an investment partnership may carry out.

The Investment Partnership Law stipulates that only profit-making organizations and non-profit making organizations if the investment activity facilitates the achievement of the charter objectives of such non-profit-making organizations may become parties to an investment partnership agreement. It is therefore prohibited for individuals including those who are individual entrepreneurs and non-profitmaking organizations for which investment activity is not a facilitation of achieving its charter objectives to become partners of an investment partnership.

It is stipulated that the number of partners in an investment partnership cannot be more than fifty.

The foregoing persons may create an investment partnership only to conduct investment activity for gaining profits. It is prohibited to consummate non-investment transactions. These transactions shall be conducted by a managing partner on his/her behalf and at his/her expense. The managing partner shall be entitled to demand that the partners reimburse the expenses incurred by him/her in connection with entering into such a transaction.

The Investment Partnership Law specifies some requirements for an investment partnership agreement that do not apply to an ordinary partnership agreement. An important requirement relates to the mandatory notarization of any and all amendments, supplementary agreements and schedules thereto. One copy of the agreement as amended and all supplementary agreements and schedules thereto is to be kept by the notary public who certifies the agreement. It is also required that an investment partnership agreement shall have a title (individual designation) containing the words "investment partnership".

The Investment Partnership Law provides for a list of material conditions of an investment partnership agreement which is much wider than that for of an ordinary partnership agreement as stipulated by the Civil Code.

It is prohibited to include a provision on creating a silent investment partnership. This provision is declared legally void. Therefore, an investment partnership may be public only.

The Investment Partnership Law introduces mandatory differentiation of partners from managing partners entailing differences in rights and duties, possible contributions of partners and the procedure for conducting the common business of the investment partnership.

Under the aegis of an investment partnership (a) managing partner(s) shall be appointed. Among managing partners there shall be one authorized partner appointed, and only a legal entity may act as such partner (this rule is not applicable to managing partners).

Those partners who are not managing partners have only one obligation: to contribute to the common business. They are not obliged to carry out any activity. An ordinary partnership agreement sets out an obligation for every partner to make a contribution and to participate in conducting activity.

A managing partner is obliged to make a contribution and manage common business. The law imposes additional obligations on an authorized partner and they are related to the recording of profits and expenditures, the opening of bank accounts and tax accounting.

The list of rights of partners and those of managing partners is similar. The only difference is that a managing partner is entitled to remuneration for managing common business.

Some specifics are connected to the types of property, proprietary and other rights which can be contributed as a contribution to common business. Monies, property, proprietary rights, other rights that have a monetary equivalent, professional knowledge, skills and goodwill may be contributed to the common business. However, the possibility of making a particular contribution depends on the type of partner. A non-managing partner may contribute monies only. A managing partner may contribute any of the foregoing. However, if the contribution is made in non-monetary form it is mandatory to have it assessed. In an ordinary partnership there is no such obligation.

The Investment Partnership Law establishes a legitimate interest and a legitimate penalty interest as a sanction for the improper performance of an obligation on contribution. There is no legitimate penalty interest for the failure to perform an obligation on contribution established for an ordinary partnership.

As far as it relates to an investment partnership, it is not permitted to split common property and allot a share in kind from such property within the validity period of the investment partnership agreement.

Special rules regulating the common business of partners exist in an investment partnership. Only managing partners may manage the common business of partners. Those agreements that invest the right to manage in non-managing partners are declared void.

However, along with this rule a possibility for partners to make decisions on common business together with all other partners is provided. This rule may be exercised in the form of a joint decision or by means of forming an investment committee. Therefore, something analogous to the general meeting of participants typical for business entities is established. This right of partners may be excluded by the investment partnership agreement.

It is prohibited to advertise that the partnership carries out investment activity and to attract new partners by means of public offer.

The Civil Code sets out that an ordinary partnership may be either fixed-term or indefinite. An investment partnership can only be fixed-term.

Article 13 of the Investment Partnership Law stipulates that the validity period of an investment partnership agreement may not exceed 15 years. Even if the termination date of an investment partnership is linked to the achievement of a specific objective, it may not exceed 15 years.

This provision relates to a special rule regulating the refusal to participate. A managing partner may refuse to participate in an investment partnership agreement only if all the other partners agree. As a general rule, it is not permitted for a non-managing partner to refuse to become a party to an investment partnership agreement at all (in respect of a non-managing partner it is possible to otherwise provide in an investment partnership agreement; the provisions related to a managing partner may not be modified).

It is established that the agreement may be terminated or modified by judicial procedure. This requirement relates to a material breach of the agreement only, while it is permitted to claim termination of an ordinary partnership agreement for any other viable reason.

The law provides for the special protection of shares of partners from levying execution on them under claims from creditors. So an execution will be levied on a share after all the others and the consent of all the other partners is required to allot such a share in kind.

The possibility of transferring rights and obligations under an investment partnership depends upon the type of partner. A non-managing partner may transfer rights and obligations under the investment partnership agreement to third parties. A managing partner is deprived of this possibility, which contributes to the consistency of managing the investment partnership business.

Specific characteristics of investment partnerships relate to the liability of partners under the common obligations of the investment partnership. The amount of liability depends upon the status of the person to whom the partnership is liable (while in a simple partnership liability depends on the type of activity carried out).

If a person to whom an investment partnership is liable is not an entrepreneur, each partner is liable jointly for all his property. If a person to whom an investment partnership is liable is an entrepreneur, each partner is liable pro rata and within the value of his share in the common property and is not liable for his other property.

The Investment Partnership Law also stipulates that if a partner exits from an investment partnership (either voluntarily or if he is deemed to be incapable), the investment partnership agreement shall continue in force, whereas for an ordinary partnership agreement this circumstance will entail its termination. It is therefore guaranteed that an investment partnership is more stable than an ordinary partnership.

Acquisition of a Business

* by Vladimir Kilinkarov

Most transactions relating to the acquisition of a business in Russia shall be restricted either to the acquisition of interest/shares in an existing company or the purchase of assets owned by such an entity in aggregate. The foregoing mechanisms are the most popular ones, due to the fact that the said methods are strictly regulated by current Russian law. Among the less common ways of business acquisition are the sale of an enterprise as a property portfolio and the merger of a legal entity (an independent form of reorganization).

Acquisition of Interest/Shares in a Russian Entity. Merger with a Russian Entity

The acquisition of interest/shares in a Russian entity may be implemented by various means, including entering into an interest purchase agreement (in the case of a limited liability company) or a share purchase agreement (in the event of a joint-stock company), payment for shares in a foreign investor by interests/shares in the acquired business (crossholding), "exchange" of interests/shares in a Russian entity to those or other assets, etc. One may come across agreements on the alienation of a share in the share (contributed) capital of associations and partnerships, but these legal forms are not so widespread.

However, this business acquisition mechanism, as in the case of a merger ("takeover") of a target company in the course of its reorganization, entails direct or indirect "succession" when an investor becomes a transferee both for the assets that interest him and for the liabilities of the acquired entity. The difference is that in the event of the acquisition of interests/shares the purchaser becomes liable for debts only for the amount of the appropriate interests/shares, whereas in the event of a merger the successor company becomes liable for debts of the acquired legal entity to the extent of all its properties. In order to discover the risks involved, it is advisable to conduct a preliminary inventory and an extensive examination of all available financial and other documents (legal and financial due diligence) of the company, which often occupies a substantial amount of time and expense.

It should also be noted that in the event of the purchase of interest in a limited liability company, and also in the event of the acquisition of shares in a joint-stock company or a share in the share (contributed) capital of a economic partnership, the participants of the LLC (shareholders of the JSC, partners in a partnership) in question, provided that it is stipulated in the company charter (for a partnership - unless otherwise stipulated in the partnership management agreement) the company (partnership) itself shall exercise a pre-emptive right in respect of the corresponding interest/shares. There is a strict legal procedure for the implementation of this mechanism, and a breach of this procedure may result in a situation where the respective participants of the LLC (shareholders of the JSC) are entitled to claim transfer of the rights and obligations of the purchaser to them in court.

In addition, the LLC charter may not permit alienation of participatory interest in its charter capital in favor of third persons or provide for the prior consent of other participants in the company or the company itself on the alienation of participatory interests in favor of one or more participants in the company. The partnership management agreement may provide for different procedures for obtaining its partners' consent on the transfer of a share in the share (contributed) capital of the partnership to third persons, depending on the grounds for such transfer and other circumstances.

It should be taken into account that a transaction on the alienation of a participatory interest (share) in the charter capital (share (contributed) capital) of an LLC (economic partnership) should be notarized.

At the same time, in the event of the acquisition of interests/shares in a business entity (economic partnership), that entity remains operable: it retains its assets and personnel; it is not required to obtain new approvals and licenses, which often take up more time than the business purchase transaction itself. The use of this mechanism may be quite profitable in financial terms, since the market value of the target company's property portfolio decreases by the amount of indebtedness of this company to third parties.

In order to take advantage of the possibility of reorganizing a Russian LLC or JSC by way of a merger with an existing business as provided for by Russian law, it is necessary to have one's own LLC or JSC in Russia, since it is not permitted to merge a Russian entity with a foreign one. In most cases, this circumstance leads to the application of a takeover mechanism within one holding company or group of Russian companies.

Employment Aspects

In accordance with Article 75 of the RF Labor Code, in the event of the change of ownership of a company's properties, the new owner is entitled to terminate the employment agreement with the executive of the company, his/her deputy and the chief accountant within three months from the date when he/she obtains the property right. The change of ownership of a company's properties is not regarded as grounds for terminating employment agreements with other employees of the company.

At the same time, it should be taken into account that, in accordance with Article 181 of the RF Labor Code, if an employment agreement with the executive of the company, his/her deputy and the chief accountant is terminated owing to the change of ownership of the company's properties, the new owner is obliged to pay compensation to the aforementioned employees in the amount of not less than three average monthly salaries. Higher compensation may be provided for in the employment agreement, so in the course of preparation for the transaction relating to the acquisition of a company it is advisable, inter alia, to analyze the employment agreements entered into with the executive of the company, his/her deputy and the chief accountant in order to establish whether they include provisions for increased compensation (the so-called "golden parachute").

Acquisition of Certain Assets of a Company

If an investor has the time and the desire to start a business in Russia from scratch, or if his/her top priority is not to acquire a real and operable business but to establish control over a certain asset/group of assets, such as real estate properties or intellectual property, such an investor should consider purchasing this real estate or business as a property portfolio.

In the case of real estate property, and even more so in the case of intellectual property, it should be understood that state registration of such transactions may require more time than the entering of the respective changes in the Unified State Register of Legal Entities (in the event of the acquisition of interest in the charter capital of a LLC) or the shareholders register (in the event of the acquisition of shares in a JSC). In addition, the purchaser of such assets will have to pay the possessor the market value for them, which may not be reduced in the event of existence of debts owed by the possessor. Nevertheless, the use of such mechanisms does not give rise to the risks usually associated with the liabilities of purchased companies (including hidden liabilities). In this case, no large-scale and expensive checks are required: it is necessary only to conduct due diligence of the title-establishing and title-confirming documents relating to the property, so substantially reducing the time and expense in the preparation of the transaction.

In the event of the alienation of certain assets of a Russian entity from its participants (shareholders), no pre-emptive right arises. However, it should be noted that if an asset alienation transaction constitutes a major or non-arm's length transaction for the seller, it must be approved by a general meeting of the participants of this entity.

According to the law on LLCs and JSCs, a major transaction means a transaction (including a loan, credit, pledge or surety) or a series of related transactions conducted by the company in connection with the acquisition, alienation or possible direct or indirect alienation of its properties whose value equals twenty five per cent or more of the value of the company's property, determined on the basis of financial statements for the most recent accounting period preceding the date on which a decision on such transaction was made, unless the company's charter provides for a greater value for a major transaction. Transactions conducted by the company in the ordinary course of its business shall not be considered major transactions. In addition to the cases listed above, the company's charter may provide for other types and/or value of transaction, to which the procedure for the approval of major transactions set out in RF legislation applies.

In RF corporate legislation a non-arm's length transaction means a transaction (including a loan, credit, pledge or surety) in which a member of the board of directors (supervisory board) of a company, a person performing the functions of the sole executive body of the company or a member of the collegial executive body of the company is interested, or in which a member of the company holding together with its affiliates twenty per cent or more of the aggregate number of votes of the members of the company or persons entitled to give the company binding instructions are interested.

A major or other transaction conducted in breach of the approval requirements may be considered null and void in the event of a claim filed by the company or its participant.

The foregoing laws include several exceptions where the established procedure for the approval of major or other transactions does not apply: for example, it does not apply in the event of the transfer of the property right in the process of a company's reorganization, including consolidation and merger agreements, or in the event that the company consummating the transaction consists of the only participant which, at the same time, performs the functions of the sole executive body of that company . In addition, a company's charter may specify that no decision of a general meeting of the participants of the company and the board of directors (supervisory board) of the company is required to conduct a major transaction.

Selection of the Executive of an Acquired Company

As in the case of establishing a new business in Russia, one of the first issues arising in the course of the incorporation of a company or the acquisition of an existing business is the appointment/change of the executive of the company. The investor has to choose between:

- an individual executive or a management company;
- a Russian or expat executive.

In the first case, a management company gives the owner of the business the possibility of terminating the agreement with the management company at his/her own discretion. In the case of an individual executive, it is necessary to observe the formalities provided for by labor law and social security law. This relates, above all, to those formalities connected with the prohibition of discrimination in the event of the termination of an employment agreement and making payments to social funds. On the other hand, it is difficult to achieve the necessary level of management personalization and personal responsibility with a management company, though financial guarantees relating to the management's responsibility for losses incurred by the company as a result of mismanagement may differ depending on the standard of the management company and the individual executive.

It is essential to understand that the procedure for the employment of an executive who is neither a Russian citizen nor a person permanently resident in Russia (the holder of a so-called "residence permit") entails compliance with immigration registration requirements, obtaining permission for the company to engage foreign employees, and also the necessity for the executive himself/herself to obtain a work permit for the whole period of the employment agreement (for details see the *Employment* section below). In addition, the employment of foreign executives frequently entails the necessity of insurance against liabilities relating to mismanagement. This type of insurance is not widespread among businesses in Russia, and only insurance market leaders provide this service.

Business Restructuring

* by Maxim Avrashkov, Natalia Zelentsova

Business restructuring means the dissolution of a legal entity when its rights and obligations are transferred to other entities. Business restructuring may arise for various reasons, and in most cases it actually entails the liquidation of the original entity and the incorporation of a new one.

Based on the provisions of the RF Civil Code, five forms of restructuring can be identified: consolidation (where two and more legal entities are transformed into one), a merger (where one or several legal entities merge with another legal entity), a demerger (where a legal entity is divided into two or more legal entities), a spin-out (where one or two legal entities are detached from a legal entity, and the legal entity from which the new legal entities have been detached continues to operate) and a transformation (where legal entity changes one form of legal entity's incorporation to another, e.g. partnership to LLC or LLC to JSC). It should be noted that restructuring of the legal entity with a simultaneous combination of its various forms is permitted by law.

The foregoing types of restructuring may be conventionally divided into two groups.

The first group includes **demergers and spin-outs**. In both these cases the restructuring of a legal entity is carried out either at the discretion of its founders (participants) or its corporate body authorized to carry out such an action by its foundation documents, or irrespective of the wishes of the legal entity it may be restructured upon a resolution of the authorized state body. A timescale for the restructuring shall be defined in this resolution. If the founders (participants), the body authorized by them for this purpose or the corporate body of the legal entity fail to carry out the restructuring within the agreed timescale, a court, at the behest of the authorized state body, shall appoint an court-appointed manager of the legal entity who will be instructed to carry out the restructuring. The court-appointed manager shall be vested with the rights of business affairs administration.. In accordance with the task assigned to the manager, he/she shall prepare a transfer act and constitutional documents of the resulting legal entity (legal entities). The transfer act and constitutional documents shall be approved by the court and this approval shall be deemed the necessary grounds for state registration of the resulting legal entity.

The second group includes **consolidations, mergers and transformations**. In the event of these forms of restructuring, the RF Civil Code permits legally admissible cases where company restructuring may be deemed possible only with the consent of the authorized state bodies (see below).

As far as document connected to the restructuring and constituting the grounds for legal succession of the legal entities are concerned, a transfer act is prepared. The transfer act shall determine to which party particular rights and obligations shall be transferred. It is necessary to include all the obligations of the restructured legal entity into the transfer act, including those for which the maturity date has not yet fallen, and also obligations which the restructured company disputes. The said document shall be approved by the persons who adopted the resolution on the restructuring.

A legal entity shall be deemed to be restructured, with the exception of cases of restructuring in the form of a merger, from the moment of the state registration of the resulting legal entities. In the event of the restructuring of a legal entity in the form of a merger, it shall be considered as restructured from the moment a record on the termination of activity of the merged legal entity is entered in the unified state register of legal entities.

Business Restructuring and Protection of Competition

Federal Law No. 135 "On Protection of Competition" of 26 July 2006 provides for cases where restructuring in the form of consolidations and mergers may be carried out only with the prior consent of the antimonopoly body.

The same law provides for the mandatory division of business entities if their incorporation has led or may lead to restriction of competition, including as a result of the creation or strengthening of a dominant position. A commercial organization incorporated without the prior consent of the antimonopoly body, including as a result of the consolidation or merger of commercial organizations in cases set forth in the foregoing law, shall be liquidated or restructured in the form of a demerger or spin-out judicially at the behest of the antimonopoly body. A court decision on the mandatory division of a commercial organization or the spin-out of one or several commercial organizations from a commercial organization shall be made in order to develop competition, provided that it is possible to separate the structural subdivisions of a commercial organization; or there is no technological correlation between the structural subdivisions of a commercial organization (in particular, where thirty per cent or less of the volume of production, performed work or rendered services of the structural subdivision are consumed by other structural subdivisions of the commercial organization); or if there is a possibility for independent activity on the respective market for the legal entities incorporated in the course of the restructuring.

Mandatory division or spin-out shall be carried out by the owner or a body authorized by the owner, taking into account the requirements provided for by the said decision and within a timescale determined by the said decision, which may not be less than six months.

Guarantees of the Rights of Creditors

The RF Civil Law provides for special regulation of issues relating to guarantees of the rights of creditors of a restructured legal entity.

Within three working days from the date of a resolution on restructuring, a legal entity shall be obliged to notify in writing the governmental body dealing with the registration of legal entities concerning the commencement of the restructuring procedure, specifying the type of restructuring. Based on this notification, the state body shall enter the appropriate record in the unified state register of legal entities. Thereupon the legal entity shall twice publish a notice on its restructuring in the mass media, the second being published a month after the first. The notice shall contain, in particular, information on the procedure and conditions for creditors to present their claims. A creditor of a legal entity, if his/her claim arose prior to the first publication of the notice on restructuring, shall be entitled to early discharge of the respective obligation by the debtor in court, and if such early discharge is not feasible – to claim termination of the obligation and reimbursement of the losses connected therewith.

The claim of the creditor does not suspend the restructuring procedure, but such a claim should be fulfilled before the reorganization is completed. If the creditor's claim is not fulfilled, then the reorganized legal entity, legal entities incorporated as a result of reorganization, persons who have the actual power to determine the actions of the reorganized legal entities, members of collegial bodies and the person authorized to act on behalf of the reorganized legal entity shall bear liability to the creditor if they through their actions (or inaction) contributed to occurrence of the consequences for the creditor.

The mentioned guarantees of the rights of creditors shall not apply in the case of reorganization in the form of reconstruction.

Insolvency

* by Sergey Bakeshin

General Description of Legal Regulation

The main legal act regulating insolvency (bankruptcy) in Russia is the Federal Law "On Insolvency (Bankruptcy)" No. 127-FZ of 26 October 2002.

According to Russian law, insolvency (bankruptcy) is the inability of a debtor to satisfy in full the claims of its creditors relating to monetary obligations and/or to perform his/her obligation to effect mandatory payments, as confirmed by a court. Cases on bankruptcy of organizations and individual entrepreneurs are considered be commercial courts at their location. Cases on bankruptcy of citizens those who are not individual entrepreneurs are considered be courts of general jurisdiction at their location.

Rules on bankruptcy of citizens who are not individual entrepreneurs come into legal force from 01 July 2015.

Legal entities of the following legal forms may not be declared bankrupt: state enterprises, institutions, political parties and religious organizations. State corporations and companies may be declared bankrupts if permitted by laws governing their incorporation. Law on creating a fund may prohibit declaring it a bankrupt.

Russian insolvency law tends to act for the benefit of the debtor. The procedures provided for therein are aimed at the restoration of the debtor's solvency rather than at the prompt disbursement of the creditors' claims. However, the Russian bankruptcy institution as such is not so effective: in most cases, bankruptcy of legal entities results in their liquidation.

Parties to Bankruptcy Proceedings

The following parties participate in bankruptcy proceedings: the debtor, a bankruptcy manager, bankruptcy creditors, authorized bodies, government authorities and local authorities in cases specified by law, and a person granting security for financial recovery.

Bankruptcy creditors are creditors to whom the debtor has monetary obligations (with the exception of authorized bodies, citizens to whom the debtor is liable for causing damage to life or health, moral damage, is liable to pay remuneration as to the authors of intellectual property and founders (participants) of the debtor based on liabilities incurred as a result of this participation).

The authorized bodies are the federal executive body presenting claims for the payment of mandatory payments (including taxes) and claims of the Russian Federation in respect of monetary obligations, executive bodies of constituent territories of the Russian Federation, and local government authorities that have filed claims related to monetary obligations to constituent territories of the Russian Federation and municipalities accordingly. The authorized federal body is the Federal Tax Service.

The key figure in bankruptcy proceedings is the bankruptcy manager. His/her authority varies depending on the applicable bankruptcy procedure: from an analysis of the debtor's activities and the preparation of a report on the possibility of restoring his/her solvency to total management of the debtor's activities. Any citizen with a degree and executive experience who has passed a special exam and is a member of one of the self-regulating organizations of bankruptcy managers may act as the bankruptcy manager.

A bankruptcy creditor (indebtedness of debtor-organization to whom is not less than 300 000 rubles and in the case creditor is not a credit institution is confirmed by a decision of the court), an authorized body or the debtor may initiate bankruptcy proceedings. In some cases the debtor is obliged to file a bankruptcy petition to the court; the non-fulfillment of this obligation may lead to the responsibility of the debtor's executive officer or the owners of the business.

Basic information on bankruptcy is published in official media as well as included in the Federal Register of Information on Bankruptcy (*see www.bankrot.fedresurs.ru*).

Bankruptcy Procedures

In the case of bankruptcy of a legal entity, such procedures as supervision, financial recovery, external management, receivership proceedings, settlement agreements and other procedures provided for by law shall apply.

The purpose of the **supervision** procedure is to analyze the financial condition of the debtor and to compile a register of the creditors' claims. After the introduction of supervision, an interim manager shall publish a notice about it, and within one month from the date of the publication of this notice the creditors are entitled to file their claims. The creditors may file their claims later, but in that case such claims shall be considered only after the move to the subsequent procedure. Based on the court's ruling, the said claims shall be entered in a register of claims. The interim manager shall draw up a report of his activities, including an indication of the possibility or impossibility of restoring the debtor's solvency and the expediency of further bankruptcy proceedings.

After the introduction of supervision, enforcement of the debtor's property shall be suspended. New monetary claims on the debtor may be filed only within the framework of the bankruptcy proceedings (with the exception of current payments, *i.e.* obligations, which arose after the date when the petition declaring the debtor bankrupt was accepted). A number of limitations relating to the debtor's activity shall be introduced.

The purpose of the **financial recovery** procedure is the restoration of the debtor's solvency and the clearance of his debts in accordance with an approved repayment schedule. Control over the course of implementation of the financial recovery plan and the schedule for the clearance of debts shall be exercised by the bankruptcy manager.

In the event of the debtor clearing his debts in accordance with the schedule or ahead of it, the bankruptcy proceedings shall be terminated. If the repayment schedule is not adhered to, the court of arbitration shall institute external management or receivership proceedings.

The purpose of **external management** is to restore the solvency of the debtor. An external manager is in charge of all affairs of the debtor in a case of external management. A moratorium on the meeting of creditors' claims is introduced. The external manager devises and the creditors' meeting approves an external management plan, which may involve reorientation of production, liquidation of unprofitable businesses, recovery of receivable debts, sale of part of the debtor's assets, assignment of claims of the debtor, performance of the debtor's obligations by a third party, increase of the charter capital of the debtor by means of contributions by participants and third parties, placement of additional common shares of the debtor, sale of the debtor's business, replacement of the debtor's assets, and other measures for the restoration of the debtor's solvency.

External management may be concluded by the termination of the bankruptcy proceedings (if all creditors' claims have been met), commencement of settlement with creditors (if the debtor's solvency has been restored), initiation of receivership proceedings or entering into a settlement agreement.

Receivership proceedings shall be initiated if the debtor is declared bankrupt for the purposes of adequate satisfaction of the creditors' claims. A bankruptcy receiver shall manage the activities of a debtor who has been declared bankrupt. The bankruptcy receiver shall sell the debtor's property at auction.

Funds owned by the debtor and received as a result of the sale of his/ her property shall be used for meeting creditors' claims in the following order of priority:

Claims for current payments shall be met out of turn. First of all, claims relating to compensation for harm caused to life or health and compensation for moral damage shall be met. Secondly, demands relating to the payment of severance benefit, payments to persons who are working or have worked according to an employment agreement and payment of remuneration to the authors of intellectual property shall be settled. Thirdly, settlements with other creditors shall be effected. The claims of creditors in each tier shall be met after all the claims filed by the creditors of the preceding tier have been met in full. Claims of creditors relating to obligations secured by pledge of the debtor's property shall be met out of turn from the value of the subject of the pledge.

If a third party (for example, the founder) discharges all the debtor's liabilities, the court shall terminate the bankruptcy proceedings and the debtor shall no longer be considered bankrupt. In other cases, after the completion of settlements with the creditors, the court passes a ruling on the termination of the receivership proceedings and a record on the liquidation of the debtor shall be entered in the Unified State Register of Legal Entities.

At any stage of the bankruptcy proceedings the debtor, his/her bankruptcy creditors and authorized bodies shall be entitled to enter into a **settlement agreement**, subject to the approval of the court. The settlement agreement specifies the procedure and term for the carrying out of the debtor's monetary obligations.

Special Characteristics of the Bankruptcy of Certain Parties

Russian law provides for a specific bankruptcy procedure for credit institutions, insurance agencies, professional participants of the securities market and other financial organizations. Government bodies and local authorities are vested with wider powers within the framework of the bankruptcy of town-forming organizations, other organizations in which more than 5,000 people are employed, strategic enterprises and organizations, natural monopoly holders. In the case of the bankruptcy of agricultural organizations the seasonal nature of their activities and the target purpose of their property shall be taken into account. In the case of the developer's bankruptcy participants of the construction project having monetary claims or claims to handover of living premises to developer are vested with special rights. A simplified procedure shall be applied towards the bankruptcy of liquidated debtors, absent debtors, specialized societies and mortgage agents and no supervision, financial recovery or external management shall apply to them.

In terms of citizens bankruptcy the following procedures shall apply: debts restructuring (restructuring plan for no longer than 3 years and other restructuring conditions are confirmed by court considering a case), assets selling (in the case of failure to provide court with debts restructuring plan or its cancellation as well as if court refuses to confirm the plan a citizen shall be declared bankrupt) and settlement agreement. Case on bankruptcy of citizen can be initiated if claimed amount is not less than 500 000 rubles.

Upon completion of settlements with creditors citizen, declared bankrupt, is released from further performance of creditors' claims. At the same time, some negative legal consequences for citizen shall apply. Thus, from the date of recognition of citizen as bankrupt he/she may not hold positions in management bodies of a legal entity (participate in management of a legal entity in other way) for three years as well as to take credits and loans without reference to the fact of the bankruptcy for five years.

For individual entrepreneurs consequences of declaring their bankruptcy are even more strictly: a bankrupt businessman can not be registered as an individual entrepreneur for one year from the date of recognition of his/her bankruptcy (citizen loses the state registration as an individual entrepreneur since the recognition of his/her bankruptcy). In the case of second bankruptcy the citizen is not entitled to carry out business activities and hold positions in management bodies of companies for five years.

Regulation of Business Activity

* by Sergey Bakeshin, Artur Osipov

The following forms of the state regulation of entrepreneurial activity are of particular importance in setting up and conducting a business in Russia:

- state registration of legal entities and individual entrepreneurs (see the *Setting up a new business* section);
- licensing;
- participation in self-regulating organizations;
- accreditation;
- notification-based and authorization-based procedure for conducting specific activities;
- certification;
- customs regulation (see the *Customs regulation* section);
- tax regulation (see the *Taxation* section)
- foreign trade regulation;
- customs control;
- export control;
- antimonopoly control.

Licensing

In the RF it is required to obtain a license to carry out some types of activity, in accordance with the Federal Law "On the Licensing of Certain Types of Activity" no. 99-FZ of 8 May 2011.

A license is a special permit to carry out a specific type of activity subject to mandatory compliance with the licensing requirements and conditions issued by a licensing body in favor of a legal entity or individual entrepreneur. The main principles of licensing include: ensuring a common economic space on RF territory, establishing a single list of licensable types of activity, a uniform procedure, requirements and conditions, and compliance with law. In connection with the foregoing it may be concluded that the introduction of licensing does not contradict the constitutional principle of free economic activity.

Licensable types of activity are types of activity which may cause harm to the rights, lawful interests and health of citizens, the defense and security of the state or the cultural heritage of peoples of the Russian Federation, and which may not be regulated in any other way but by licensing, including the operation of fire and explosion dangerous and chemically hazardous production facilities, drug manufacture, carriage of passengers by inland water, sea, air and rail transport, activity related to the organization and carrying out of gambling in betting offices and pari-mutuel, private detective and security activity, rendering of communication services, pharmaceutical activities and others (according to the foregoing law as of 1 May 2015 there are 50 licensable activities all in all).

A licensable type of activity may be carried out only by the legal entity or individual entrepreneur obtaining the license. The right based on the license forms part of the legal capacity of the license holder and unlike a legal right it may not be transferred to other persons.

The validity period of a license may not be less than five years. In order to obtain a license, a license applicant shall submit or present a license application and requisite documents to the relevant licensing body. The licensing body shall make a decision on the issue or refusal of a license within a period not exceeding forty-five days from the date of receipt of the application and supporting documents

If a license holder breaches the requirements and conditions of a license, he/she may be held administratively liable in accordance with the procedure stipulated by the RF Administrative Violations Code, and the license may be suspended. If a license holder fails to remedy the breach of requirements and conditions that resulted in the administrative suspension of activity, the licensing body shall be obliged to seek cancellation of the license in court. A license can be cancelled by court decision.

As far as civil law consequences are concerned, all transactions entered into by an entity (entrepreneur) in the absence of a license may be held invalid. The entity may be liquidated judicially for engaging in business without a license.

Specific laws provide for licensing of nuclear energy use, production and circulation of ethyl alcohol, alcoholic beverages and alcohol containing products, state secrets protection activities, and various financial activities (the same of credit institutions, bidding process organizers, professional securities market participants, investment and pension funds, depositories as well as clearing and insurance activities).

In recent times the number of licensable types of activity has shown a tendency to decrease. However, this does not mean that the state refrains from the regulation of some or other types of entrepreneurial activity. Licensing is being supplanted by alternative means of regulation – participation in self-regulating organizations, accreditation, obtaining permits to engage in specific activities.

Self-Regulating Organizations

Membership-based nonprofit-making organizations that unite entities carrying out entrepreneurial activity due to their common field of production of commodities (works, services) or market of produced commodities (works, services) or combining entities that carry out professional activity of a certain type are deemed to be self-regulating organizations.

In Russia the procedure for the establishment and operation of a self-regulating organization, its main goals and tasks are regulated by Federal Law No. 315-FZ "On Self-Regulating Organizations" of 1 December 2007 and by federal laws governing the relevant type of activity. The main objective for establishing self-regulating organizations is to shift functions involving control and supervision over activity of entities in a specific sphere from the state onto market participants themselves.

In a wide number of cases federal laws provide mandatory participation of entities that carry out specific entrepreneurial and professional activity in self-regulating organizations. Some types of activity not requiring the issuance of a license may be conducted only if the entity is a member of a self-regulating organization in a certain field (for example, design, construction, audit, appraisal, activity of bankruptcy administrators, *etc.*).

There are some activities where self-regulation is provided by law, however membership in a self-regulating organization is not a must for conducting such an activity (for example, advertising)

Accreditation

Laws governing specific activities can set out a procedure for mandatory or voluntary accreditation. In particular, accreditation is provided for:

* representative offices and branches of foreign legal entities;
* legal entities, individual entrepreneurs performing conformity assessment activities;
* legal entities, individual entrepreneurs engaged by bodies authorized to exercise state control (supervision), bodies of municipal control for carrying out control measures;
* experts, expert organizations engaged by federal executive authorities for exercise of separate powers;
* in the field of atomic energy use;
* carrying out non-state expert examination of project documentation and (or) non-state expert examination of results of engineering investigations;
* healthcare organizations for the clinical trial of drugs intended for medical use;
* organizations dealing with the administration of rights on a collective basis;
* sport federations;
* educational establishments;
* entities engaged in the field of ensuring the uniformity of measurements;
* certification bodies and testing laboratories (centers);
* operators of vehicle inspection;
* specialized organizations in the sphere of transport security.
* rating agencies;
* certification centers;

At present Federal Law No. 412-ФЗ "On accreditation in national accreditation system" dd. 28.12.2013 is in force in the Russian Federation.

Notification-Based and Authorization-Based Procedures for Conducting Specific Activities

When individual entrepreneurs and legal entities carry out specific activities (for example, hotel services, wholesale and retail, some kinds of transportation, production of specific products, *etc.*) in Russia, they should **notify** the territorial subdivisions of the authorized federal executive body. For further details please see the *Setting up a new business. Joint ventures* sections.

There are some activities which, although not licensable, are subject to various requirements, namely: epidemiological, sanitary, ecological, fire safety, traffic code, safety, *etc*. In order to carry out such activities it is required to obtain a relevant **permit** (construction, reconstruction, capital repair, hazardous substance emission, employment of foreign nationals, import (export) of commodities to (or from) a special economic zone, *etc*.). Such permits are issued by the executive authorities and officials. These permits serve as the grounds for conducting the respective activity. The absence of a permit shall entail administrative and criminal liability.

Certification

In accordance with Federal Law "On Technical Regulation" (No. 184-FZ of 27 December 2002) (hereinafter referred to as "Law 184-FZ"), certification is the form of confirmation by a certification body of the compliance of objects with the requirements of technical regulations, provisions of standards, sets of rules or terms of agreements. In the context of a free market economy, certification is the principal means of guaranteeing the compliance of products with the requirements of legal documentation.

The principles and rules of technical regulations are also specified in international agreements, concluded within the European Economic Community.

Technical Regulation means a document adopted under the aegis of an international treaty of the Russian Federation, ratified in compliance with the procedure set out by the legislation of the Russian Federation or an intergovernmental agreement entered into as provided by the legislation of the Russian Federation, a federal law or an order of the President of the Russian Federation or a decree of the Government of the Russian Federation and establishing the binding requirements to items subject to technical regulation (items, including buildings, constructions and structures or design (including survey), production, construction, assembling, setting up, operation processes related to the items' requirements).

The institution of technical requirements is designed to replace the institution of state standards which also contains mandatory requirements on the manufactured products.

Technical regulations establish the minimum necessary requirements relating to emission, biological, explosion, mechanical, fire, production, thermal, chemical, electrical, nuclear and radiation safety, electromagnetic compatibility to the extent related to ensuring the safe operation of tools and equipment and uniformity of measurements, as well as other types of safety, for the purposes pertaining to the adoption of specific technical regulation.

A technical regulation shall contain a list and/or a description of items subject to technical regulation, requirements to them and rules for their identification for the purposes of application of the technical regulation as well as rules and forms for the conformity assessment specified subject to the degree of risk, deadlines for conformity assessment in respect of each item subject to technical regulation and/ or requirements to terminology, packaging, marking or labeling or rules for their manufacture (Article 7 of Law 184-FZ).

Certification can be either mandatory or voluntary. In compliance with Decree of the Government of the Russian Federation "On Approval of the Uniform List of Products Subject to Mandatory Certification and the Uniform List of Products the Conformity of Which Is to Be Confirmed in the Form of Adoption of a Declaration of Conformity" No 982 of 1 December 2009 the following products are subject to mandatory certification: weapons, radiation system, electric energy in public electric grids, railroad rails, railroad equipment and rolling stock, pipes for gas pipelines, *etc*. Those products in respect of which it is obligatory to issue a declaration of conformity are not subject to mandatory certification. Such products, specifically, include lubricant (petroleum) oils, liquefied gas, metallic housewares, mineral fertilizers, *etc*.

A document issued in accordance with the system of certification rules for the purposes of confirmation of the compliance of the certified products with the established requirements, applicable standards and rules (GOST, GOST R, GOST R MEK, GOST R ISO) is a **certificate of conformity**. Possession of this certificate assists consumers in choosing adequate products and acts as a definite guarantee of their quality. Certificates of conformity are issued by certification bodies (legal entities or individual entrepreneurs properly accredited to carry out certification work). Mandatory certification shall be carried out on the basis of an agreement with the applicant. Certification schemes applicable to the certification of certain types of products shall be established by the corresponding technical regulations..

Voluntary confirmation of conformity shall be initiated by an applicant on the basis of an agreement between the applicant and the certification body. Voluntary confirmation of conformity can be made with respect to:

products, processes of production, operation, storage, transportation, sale and disposal of a work or service as well as other things subject to specific requirements established by standards, voluntary certification systems and agreements. Voluntary confirmation of conformity may be carried out in order to establish conformity with national standards, standards of organizations, sets of rules, voluntary certification systems, terms and conditions of agreements. Items certified under the voluntary certification system may be marked with a mark of conformity with the voluntary certification system.

Foreign Trade Regulation

State regulation of foreign trade is carried out in compliance with the international treaties of the Russian Federation, Federal Law "On the Fundamentals of Foreign Trade Regulation" No. 164-FZ of 8 December 2003 (hereinafter referred to as "Law 164-FZ") and other regulations of the Russian Federation.

According to Article 2 of Law 164-FZ, **foreign trade** means activity focused on the consummation of foreign trade transactions involving products, services, information and intellectual property. Therefore, the import and export of goods (foreign trade in goods), rendering services (performance works) from the territory of the Russian Federation to the territory of a foreign country or vice versa, rendering services in the territory of the Russian Federation to a foreign customer or rendering services in the territory of a foreign country to a Russian customer, or rendering services by a Russian service provider in the territory of a foreign country or rendering services by a foreign service provider in the Russian Federation (foreign trade in services), or transfer of exclusive rights to IPs or granting the right to use thereof by a Russian person to a foreign person or by a foreign person to a Russian person (foreign trade in IPs) are subject to foreign trade regulation.. Foreign trade in information may be conducted either within the framework of foreign trade in goods (provided that such information forms a part of such goods), or under foreign trade in IPs (provided that such information is transferred as an IP right), or under foreign trade in services in other instances. State foreign trade regulation may be carried out using only the following methods:

* customs and tariffs regulation;
* non-tariff regulation;
* bans and restrictions of foreign trade in services and IPs;
* economic and administrative measures facilitating foreign trade development.

Customs and tariffs regulation is performed in order to protect the domestic market and stimulate the economy in compliance with the international agreements of the Customs Union member states and the laws of the Russian Federation For more details please see the *Customs Regulation* section below.

Non-tariff regulation in the area of foreign trade in goods may be carried out only in cases expressly set out in Law 164-FZ. Non-tariff regulation involves imposing bans or quantitative restrictions on the export of essential commodities (for example, milk, wheat, flour, sunflower oil) and on the import of agricultural products and aquatic biological recourses in exceptional instances. These restrictions apply regardless of the country of origin of the commodities and can be introduced by the Government of the Russian Federation for a period not exceeding six months.

As a general rule foreign trade is conducted **without a license**, but an authorization-based procedure may be introduced in some cases: for example, when temporary quantitative restrictions are imposed on the export or import of specific commodities, the exclusive right to export and/or import certain types of goods is granted or in connection with the performance of international obligations by the Russian Federation.

Goods originating from a foreign country and services rendered by foreign service providers shall enjoy treatment not less favorable than applicable to analogous Russian goods and services. It is not permitted to set differentiated tax and duty rates (other than customs import duties) depending on the country of origin. Foreign commodities and services are subject to the same requirements (technical, sanitary, *etc.*) as analogous Russian commodities and services. Therefore, foreign commodities and services are subject to **national legal treatment**.

One of the measures for the regulation of foreign trade is the introduction of **special safeguard, anti-dumping and countervailing measures** relating to the import of goods in order to protect the economic interests of Russian manufacturers. Administrative measures of regulation may be introduced under the international treaties of the Russian Federation and federal laws based on the national interest for the purposes specified in law. For instance, according to a decision made by the Government of the Russian Federation a special anti-dumping duty may be imposed on goods if their export price (i.e. the price at which the goods are imported to the customs territory of the Russian Federation) is lower than the comparable price for similar goods established in the ordinary course of trade in analogous goods on the market of the foreign country from which the goods are exported (see Federal Law "On Special Safeguard, Anti-Dumping and Countervailing Measures Related to the Import of Goods" No. 165-FZ of 8 December 2003).

Another way of regulating foreign trade is the imposition of **bans and restrictions on the foreign trade in goods, services and intellectual properties** in order to implement measures required for the Russian Federation to adhere to international sanctions in compliance with the UN Charter. The restrictions may also be introduced in order to maintain the balance-of-payment equilibrium of the Russian Federation or in connection with customs control measures (for example, in the event of a decrease in currency reserves or for the prevention of a material decrease in currency reserves of the Russian Federation).

Temporary restrictions on foreign trade in goods, services, intellectual properties may be introduced in the form of countermeasures **(retorsion)** if a foreign country conducts unlawful actions or fails to perform its international obligations: if a foreign country fails to observe its obligations to the Russian Federation under international treaties, fails to provide adequate and efficient protection of rights and lawful interests of Russian persons in that country, for example, a protection against anticompetitive activity of other persons, fails to carry out reasonable actions to combat illegal activities of individuals or legal entities of that country in the Russian Federation.

Control over the observance of foreign trade regulation is exercised by the authorized state authorities. For the offenses committed civil, administrative or criminal proceedings may be initiated against guilty persons under the legislation of the Russian Federation.

Possibility of introduction of interim measures as a quick reaction to internationally wrongful act or unfriendly act of foreign state or its authority and official that threaten security and interests of the RF or injure rights and freedoms of the RF citizens is specified by Federal Law "On Special Economic Measures" (No. 281-FZ of 30 December 2006). Prohibition against certain actions as for foreign state and (or) foreign organizations and citizens as well as stateless persons permanently residing on the territory of foreign state, and (or) placing of duty to commit the actions and other restrictions are considered as special economic measures. Example of special economic measures is food sanctions introduced by Russia in the summer of 2014.

Currency Control

Currency control is also a kind of state foreign trade control exercised in order to protect the public interests of Russia.

In the Russian Federation currency control is exercised by the Government of the Russian Federation, the Central Bank of the Russian Federation and banks reporting to it, professional securities market players (currency control agents) and state authorities in accordance with Federal Law "On Currency Regulation and Currency Control" No. 173-FZ of 10 December, 2003 (hereinafter referred to as "Law 173-FZ"). Currency legislation has been recently significantly relaxed, however currency control was not totally abolished.

Currency control focuses on verifying currency regulation compliance by residents and non-residents, checking reliability of record-keeping and accounts under currency operations. In order to accomplish these tasks currency control authorities may request the necessary information on conducting currency operations, opening and maintaining of bank accounts, issue instructions to rectify breaches of law and hold offenders liable for violations in this area.

Under Russian law the following parties are deemed non-residents (Article 1 of Law 173-FZ):

- organizations incorporated under foreign law and located outside the Russian Federation;
- unincorporated organizations formed under foreign law and located outside the Russian Federation;
- branches, permanent representative offices and other autonomous or independent structural subdivisions of the foregoing non-residents located in the Russian Federation;
- foreign nationals or stateless persons, except for those living permanently in the Russian Federation on the basis of a residence permit;
- citizens of the Russian Federation recognized as permanently living in a foreign country under the laws of that country.

Currency operations between residents and non-residents and those between non-residents are unlimited, with one exception: foreign currency and checks (including traveler's checks) with a nominal value denominated in foreign currency may be sold and purchased in the Russian Federation only through authorized banks (Article 11 of Law

173-FZ). There are no restrictions imposed on the transfer of currency from Russian bank accounts to foreign bank accounts (Article 10 of Law 173-FZ).

By recent changes in the Law No. 173-ФЗ Government of the Russian Federation is entitled to oblige residents to receive revenue from foreign trade contracts in the Russian Federation currency (thus Government can define a share of such revenue and state a list of goods, works, services for which calculations in rubles are carried out, as well as a list of foreign states with residents of which specified contracts are concluded).

Law 173-FZ distinguishes residents from non-residents only for the purposes of the regulation of currency relations, not in order to worsen the position of foreign organizations. The interests of residents and non-residents are equally protected by the state.

For the purposes of currency control, both residents and non-residents conducting currency operations in the Russian Federation shall provide the authorized bodies and currency control agents with a number of documents, specifically, documents and information related to currency operations, the opening or maintenance of bank accounts, documents (drafts thereof) serving as grounds for currency operations, including agreements (contracts) and amendments thereto and/or modifications thereof, powers of attorney, extracts from the minutes of the general meeting or other management body of a legal entity, customs declarations, documents confirming the import/export to/from the Russian Federation of goods, currency of the Russian Federation, foreign currency as well as certificated domestic and foreign securities, *etc.*

The currency control mechanism is established by Instruction of the Central Bank of the Russian Federation "On the Procedure for Providing Documents and Information Connected with Currency Operations with Authorized Banks by Residents and Non-Residents, Procedure for the Issuance of Passports of Transaction, Recording of Currency Operations and Control over Their Performance by the Authorized Banks" No. 138-I of 4 June 2012 (hereinafter referred to as the "**Instruction**").

The Instruction provides for a special mechanism of control over crediting foreign currencies gained as a result of foreign trade activities to the bank accounts of residents. The requirements for drawing up documents relating to export and import operations are established.

The main currency control document is a currency operations statement However, sometimes a stricter currency control regime is provided which requires a passport of transaction (*passport sdelki*) to be issued. A passport of transaction shall be executed when a resident and non-resident enter into an agreement providing for conducting a currency operation with liabilities thereunder exceeding USD 50,000. A **passport of transaction** is a document containing information required to maintain records and accounts relating to currency operations between residents and non-residents. An agreement or an extract therefrom and other documents provided by the Instruction shall be submitted to the authorized bank together with a passport of transaction.

A passport of transaction is not required for currency operations carried out by the federal executive bodies, specially authorized by the RF Government to conduct currency operation, residents being credit institutions, non-residents being individuals who are not individual entrepreneurs and not engaged in private practice;

Criminal and administrative liability is established for a breach of the currency legislation. Criminal liability (up to imprisonment for a period of up to 3 years) is stated for violation of claims for crediting funds to a bank account for goods delivered to nonresidents, works conducted for them, services rendered for them, information and results of intellectual activity transferred to them, including exclusive rights on them, as well as for violation of claims for return to a resident's account of funds paid to nonresidents for goods not imported to the territory of the Russian Federation (not received on the territory of the Russian Federation), works not conducted, services not rendered, information and results of intellectual activity not transferred, if the amount of these funds exceeds 6 million rubles.

If the amount of such funds does not exceed 6 million rubles the organization being the resident and its officials shall be administratively liable in the form of a penalty equal to one-one hundred fiftieth of the refinancing rate of the Central Bank of the Russian Federation on the amount credited to the accounts in authorized banks in breach of the established term for each day overdue and/or to the sum ranging from three-quarters of the amount not credited to the accounts in authorized banks to the whole amount.

Opening of Bank Accounts in Banks Located Outside the Russian Federation by Residents of the Russian Federation

The currency legislation provides for special rules governing the opening of bank accounts abroad by residents of the Russian Federation (including organizations incorporated in the Russian Federation with the participation of foreign persons).

For example, residents are entitled to open accounts (deposits) in foreign currency without any restrictions only in those banks which are located in the Organization for Economic Cooperation and Development member states or Financial Action Task Force on Money Laundering (FATF) member states.

Residents shall notify the tax authorities at the place of registration of the opening (closing) of accounts (deposits) and amendments of their details within one month of, respectively, the opening (closing) or change of such accounts (deposits) in banks located outside the Russian Federation.

Residents are entitled to transfer funds from their accounts (deposits) in Russian banks or their accounts (deposits) in foreign banks to their accounts (deposits) opened in banks located outside the Russian Federation. However, residents may transfer funds to their accounts (deposits) opened in banks outside the Russian Federation from their accounts (deposits) in Russian banks only upon presenting to the authorized bank (during the first transfer) a notice from the tax authority at the place of registration of such resident on opening the account (deposit) marked as accepted, except for operations required in compliance with the foreign country's law and related to the terms and conditions of opening these accounts (deposits).

Residents being legal entities are entitled to carry out operations with funds credited to their accounts (deposits) opened in banks outside the Russian Federation without limitation, except for most currency operations between residents. Individuals being residents can conduct currency operations involving funds credited on the accounts (deposits) opened outside the Russian Federation without any restrictions save for the operations related to transferring property and rendering services in the Russian Federation.

Residents shall provide tax authorities with reports on cash flows on their accounts (deposits) in banks outside the territory of the Russian Federation with confirming bank documents attached and in the order established by the Government of the Russian Federation in coordination with the Central Bank of the Russian Federation.

The following persons are prohibited to open and maintain accounts in foreign banks: the persons filling (holding) public positions in the Russian Federation and constituent territories (regions) of the Russian Federation, position of the first deputy and deputies of the RF Prosecutor General, members of the Board of Directors of the RF

Central Bank, federal public service positions, to which people are appointed or dismissed by the RF President, the RF Government or the RF Prosecutor General, positions of the deputy heads of the federal executive bodies, positions in state corporations (companies), funds and other organizations established in the Russian Federation by virtue of the federal laws, to which people are appointed or dismissed by the RF President or the RF Government, positions of the heads of urban circles, municipal districts, spouses and minors of the said persons as well as other persons in cases provided by the federal laws.

Export Control

Export control is a comprehensive set of measures ensuring the implementation of the foreign trade procedure in respect of goods, information, works, services, results of intellectual activity (rights thereto) which may be used in the course of creating weapons of mass destruction, the means of their delivery, other weapons or military equipment or in the preparation for and carrying out of terrorist acts.

In the Russian Federation export control is exercised in compliance with Federal Law "On Export Control" No. 183-FZ of 18 July 1999.

The lists of controlled goods and technologies are approved by Orders of the President of the Russian Federation as advised by the Government of the Russian Federation. At the moment there is an effective list of double-purpose goods and technologies that may be used for creating weapons and military equipment which are subject to export control, approved by Order of the President of the Russian Federation No. 1661 of 17 December 2011. Such goods include, in particular: telecommunication equipment, pyrotechnical products, integrated microcircuits, *etc.*

In the Russian Federation export control is exercised by means of the regulation of foreign trade, including:

* identification of controlled goods and technologies, *i.e.* identifying whether specific raw materials, materials, equipment, scientific and technical information, works, services, results of intellectual activity correspond to the goods and technologies included in the foregoing list;
* an authorization-based procedure for conducting foreign trade operations with controlled goods and technologies, providing for licensing or other form of state regulation;
* customs control when conducting customs operations in respect of

controlled goods and technologies imported to/exported from the Russian Federation;

* arranging and conducting checks of compliance by Russian parties to foreign trade activity with the requirements set out by the export control legislation in respect of the procedure for carrying out foreign trade operations involving controlled goods, information, works, services, results of intellectual activity (rights thereto) and assuming measures provided by the legislation of the Russian Federation aimed at the preclusion and/or elimination of consequences of the revealed violations of the said requirements.

Trade Regulation

The principal law regulating trade regulation in Russia is Federal Law "On the Principles of State Regulation of Trade in the Russian Federation" No. 381-FZ of 28 December 2009.

This law regulates relations arising with respect to the organization and performance of trade, as well as relations between commercial entities in the course of trading. The law defines the following terms: trade types (wholesale and retail), immovable and movable retail facilities, trade networks *etc*. It also defines the powers of federal, regional and local authorities in relation to trade regulation.

The trade in food products is the most comprehensively regulated in the law. The law entitles the RF Government to establish the maximum permissible retail prices for basic food products if the increase in price for these products increases by 30% or more over a 30-day period.

The maximum fee payable by a supplier to a trading organization upon reaching specific amounts of sales of food products is 10% of the price of the goods. This fee may not be paid for the purchase of basic food products, the list of which shall be approved by the RF Government. An agreement entered into between a supplier and a trading company may not include conditions relating to other types of fee to be paid to the latter. There are deadlines for the settlement of accounts between trade companies and food suppliers, depending on the expiry date of the products.

A separate paid advertising, marketing or other promotion agreement may be entered into between a supplier and a trading company. However, it is prohibited to stipulate the conclusion of a supply agreement by entering into a paid services agreement.

It is not permitted to include in supply agreements a condition on the return of products that are not sold within a specified term; it is not permitted to engage in wholesale trade using a commission agent agreement or a mixed agreement containing elements of a commission agent agreement.

It is not permitted to purchase or rent additional outlets of a trading network whose share exceeds 25% of all sold food products expressed in monetary terms for the preceding financial year within the boundaries of a constituent territory of the Russian Federation, including within the boundaries of Moscow or St. Petersburg, a municipal district or an urban district.

The law provides for the formation of trade registers in constituent territories of the Russian Federation. The trade registers shall contain information on trading organizations and suppliers, and on the status of trade on the respective constituent territories of the Russian Federation. Submission of information for the trade register is voluntary.

Trade with consumers, *i.e.* with individuals who purchase products for purposes not related to the conducting of entrepreneurial activity is regulated by RF law "On the Protection of Consumer Rights" No. 2300-1 of 7 February 1992. It defines consumer rights relating, in particular, to obtaining information about commodities, shortages of commodities, exchange of good quality commodities that did not suit due to their style, color *etc.* The responsibility of the seller for a breach of consumer rights is established.

Special Trade Regulations Relating to Certain Types of Commodities are established by special laws or resolutions of the RF Government. In particular, it relates to the following product:

* alcoholic and alcohol-containing products;
* electric power;
* weapons;
* pharmaceutical products;
* drugs and psychotropic substances and their precursors;
* certain types of commodities (including food products; textile, knitted goods, clothes, furs and footwear; sophisticated household goods; perfumes and cosmetics; cars, motor machinery, trailers and numbered vehicle units; precious metals and jewelry; medical products; animals and plants; household cleaning products; pesticides and agrochemicals; copies of audiovisual works and phonograms, computer and database programs; construction materials and products; furniture; liquefied hydrogen gas; non-periodical publications).

Regulation of Operations with Monies and Other Property

Federal Law "On Counteraction of the Legalization (Laundering) of the Proceeds of Crime and Financing of Terrorism" No. 115-FZ of 7 August 2001 (hereinafter referred to as "Law 115-FZ") provides for a legal mechanism of the said counteraction governing operations with monies or other property carried out by organizations belonging to the types set out in the foregoing Law. Organizations to be controlled include:

- credit institutions;
- professional participants of the securities market;
- insurance and leasing companies;
- federal post service organizations;
- pawn shops;
- organizations buying up, acquiring and selling precious metals and precious stones, jewelry made of them and their scrap;
- organizations operating totalizers and bookmaker's offices as well as the same organizing and holding lotteries, totalizers (pari mutual) and other gambling activities, including those in the electronic format;
- organizations managing investment funds or non-public pension funds;
- organizations rendering mediatory services during real estate sale and purchase transactions;
- payment processors;
- commercial entities concluding factoring agreements as financial agents;
- credit consumer cooperatives;
- microlenders;
- mutual insurance companies;
- nongovernmental pension funds, which have a license for pension protection and pension insurance;
- communication operators with the right to provide services of mobile telephone communications..

The foregoing organizations must elaborate and exercise internal control rules, identify client, its representative and beneficiary. If there are no special supervisory bodies in the sphere of business of the said organizations, such organization must be registered with an authorized body, the Federal Financial Monitoring Service.

The above-mentioned entities must document and submit information on the following operations to the authorized body within three business days upon conducting of such operations subject to mandatory control:

* specific operations involving monies and movable properties to the amount equal to or exceeding RUR 600,000;
* a transaction entailing transfer of title to real estate to the amount equal to or exceeding RUR 3,000,000;
* a transaction aimed at receiving by a non-profitmaking organization of monies and/or other property from foreign states, international and foreign organizations, foreign nationals, stateless persons as well as at spending monies or other property of the mentioned organization in the amount exceeding RUR 100,000;
* transaction of crediting an account (deposit), covered (deposited) letter of credit or of debiting of an account (deposit), covered (deposited) letter of credit of economic societies which have a strategic impact for military industrial complex and safety of the Russian Federation, as well as societies which are under their direct or indirect control if its amount is equal or exceeds 50 000 000 rubles;
* a transaction involving monies or other property a party to which is an organization or individual with respect to which there is information that it/he/she is engaged in extremist activity or terrorism, or a legal entity under direct or indirect ownership or control of such organization, or person, or an individual or legal entity acting for or on behalf of such organization or person. The list of such persons shall be composed by the Federal Financial Monitoring Service and published in the official print media and on the official web-site of the service (*http://www.fedsfm.ru/documents/terr-list*).

Protection of Competition

* by Vladimir Kilinkarov

The institutional and legal principles for the protection of competition, including issues relating to the prevention and extinction of monopolistic activity and unfair competition in the Russian Federation are regulated by the Federal Law "On the Protection of Competition" No. 135-FZ of 26 July 2006 (hereinafter referred to as the "Competition Law"). The Russian antimonopoly law is quite strict; it focuses on ensuring the unity of the economic area, free movement of commodities, free business activity in the Russian Federation, protection of competition and creation of conditions conducive to the effective functioning of the commodity and financial markets.

The Competition Law covers relations connected to the protection of competition involving Russian and foreign bodies, legal entities and individuals, including individual entrepreneurs. In addition, the provisions of the Competition Law apply to agreements reached between Russian and/or foreign organizations or individuals outside the Russian Federation and acts performed by them, if such agreements are reached and the acts are performed with respect to fixed production-related assets and/or intangible assets or shares (interest) in business entities located in the Russian Federation, rights related to commercial entities operating in the Russian Federation or affect the competitive situation in Russia in other ways.

Abuse of a Dominant Position

In the Russian Federation it is prohibited for a dominating business entity (group of persons) to perform acts (or omissions) that may result in the prohibition, restriction or elimination of competition and/ or infringement of other persons' interests, including such acts as the establishment and maintenance of the monopoly of a high or low price for a commodity; the withdrawal of a commodity from circulation, if this results in an increased price for the commodity; soliciting a contractor to include terms and conditions in an agreement that are unfavorable to the contractor or irrelevant to the subject matter of the agreement, reducing or phasing out production of a commodity without economic and technological grounds, if that commodity is in demand or orders for its supply are placed and the profitable production of the commodity is possible; the refusal or avoidance of entering into an agreement with certain purchasers (customers) without economic and technological grounds in the event of the manufacturability or supply capacity of the respective commodity; the creation of discriminatory conditions; the imposition of obstacles to access to the commodity market or exit from the commodity market for other business entities *etc.*

The following shall be recognized as business entities:

1) individual entrepreneurs,
2) commercial entities,
3) non-commercial entities conducting profit-gaining activity,
4) individuals who are not registered as individual entrepreneurs but carry out profit-gaining professional activity.

A number of individuals and/or business entities shall be deemed a group of persons if they meet the specific criteria set out in the Competition Law. A group of persons is a special kind of collective subject of relations regulated by the Competition Law.

In this case a dominant position means a position of a business entity (group of persons) or several business entities (groups of persons) on the market of a specific commodity that provides the business entity (group of persons) or entities (groups of persons) with the opportunity to exercise a dominant influence over the general conditions of the circulation of that commodity on the respective commodity market and/or to remove other business entities from that commodity market and/or inhibit access to that commodity market for other business entities. The Competition Law establishes specific criteria for the recognition of the business entities (groups of persons) dominating the market.

Agreements or Concerted Actions on Limiting Competition

The Competition Law prohibits agreements between competitive business entities (both in writing and orally), if such agreements or concerted actions result or may result in the establishment or maintenance of prices (tariffs), discounts, extra charges (additional payments) or surcharges; the increase, reduction or maintenance of prices at auctions; the division of the commodity market on an area basis; the volume of sales or purchase of commodities; the assortment of commodities to be sold or the line-up of sellers or purchasers (customers); refusal to enter into agreements with specific sellers or purchasers (customers) without economic or technological grounds; reduction in or termination of the manufacture of products; refusal to enter into agreements with specific sellers or purchasers (customers).

No "vertical" agreements between business entities are permitted (an agreement between two business entities not competing with each other, under which one party purchase goods, and the other party sells goods; agency agreement shall not be considered as a vertical), if such agreements result or may result in the establishment of a resale price for the commodity (with the exception of cases where a seller fixes a maximum resale price for a purchaser), or if by such agreements the seller makes a demand not to permit the sale of the commodity of a competing business entity. This prohibition does not apply to agreements relating to the organization by the seller of the sale of commodities under the trade mark or company name of the seller or producer.

Concerted actions of competitive business entities are prohibited if such concerted actions lead to the establishment or maintenance of prices (tariffs), discounts, extra charges (additional payments) or surcharges; the increase, reduction or maintenance of prices at auctions; the division of the commodity market on an area basis; the volume of sales or purchase of commodities; the assortment of commodities to be sold or the line-up of sellers or purchasers (customers); refusal to enter into agreements with specific sellers or purchasers (customers) without economic or technological grounds; reduction in or termination of the manufacture of products; refusal to enter into agreements with specific sellers or purchasers (customers), unless such refusal is expressly provided by federal laws.

Other agreements between business entities or other concerted actions by business entities are also prohibited if such agreements or concerted actions result or may result in the restriction of competition.

However, written "vertical" agreements (except for "vertical" agreements between financial institutions) are permitted if such agreements constitute franchising agreements or if the share of each party thereto on any commodity market does not exceed twenty per cent.

Acts (omissions) of business entities, agreements and concerted actions between them may be considered permissible if such acts (omissions), agreements and concerted actions, transactions and other actions do not create the possibility for individuals to eliminate competition on the respective commodity market, do not impose restrictions on their participants or third parties that do not correspond to the objectives of such acts (omissions), agreements and concerted actions, transactions and other actions, and if they result or may result in the improvement of production, the sale of commodities or the stimulation of technical and economic progress or an increase in the competitiveness of commodities of Russian origin on the world commodity market, and the obtaining of advantages (benefits) by purchasers comparable with the advantages (benefits) derived by business entities as a result of acts (omissions), agreements and concerted actions, and transactions.

Unfair Competition

No unfair competition is permitted, *i.e.* any acts of business entities (group of persons) intended to gain advantages in the course of the performance of business are against Russian Federation law, as well as being in contradiction of good business practice and the demands of honesty, reasonableness and equitableness, and which have caused or may cause losses to other competitive business entities, or have resulted or may result in damage to their business reputation.

In particular, the following actions are considered to be unfair competition:

1) the dissemination of false, inaccurate or distorted information that may cause losses to a business entity or harm its business reputation;
2) misrepresentations relating to the nature, method or place of production, consumer properties, quality and quantity of goods, or to their producers;
3) the inappropriate comparison of commodities manufactured or sold by the manufacturer or seller of such commodities to those manufactured or sold by other business entities;
4) the sale, exchange or other introduction into circulation of a commodity, if in the course of such a sale, exchange or other introduction into circulation one has unlawfully used the intellectual property or means of individualization of a legal entity, the means of individualization of products, work or services equated to intellectual property;
5) the illegal obtaining, use or disclosure of information constituting commercial, official or other secrets protected by law.

Unfair competition relating to the obtaining and use of the exclusive right to the means of individualization of a legal entity, the means of individualization of products, works or services is also prohibited.

Acts and Actions (Omissions) of Authorities Restricting Competition

The Competition Law expressly prohibits acts and actions (omissions) on the restriction of competition, agreements or concerted actions by federal executive bodies, governmental authorities of the constituent territories of the Russian Federation, local authorities, other bodies or entities operating as the foregoing authorities taking part in provision of state or municipal services and state social funds, the Central Bank of the Russian Federation.

Government Control of Economic Concentration

Since some transactions and other actions may have a significant influence on competition ("economic concentration"), the Competition Law sets out situations where the incorporation and reorganization of commercial entities and transactions involving their shares (interest) and assets require the prior consent of the antimonopoly body.

For example, in the event of the consolidation or merger of commercial entities, the necessity of obtaining the prior consent of the antimonopoly body depends on the total value of their assets and the total proceeds of the parties to the reorganization (groups of persons) (more than 7 billion rubles and 10 billion rubles respectively). In the case of the incorporation of a commercial entity, the necessity for prior consent also depends on its total assets (more than 7 billion rubles) or the total proceeds of its founders (group of persons) (more than 10 billion rubles).

In addition, consent of the antimonopoly body is required if one of the parties to the transaction parties is entered in the register of business entities (with the exception of financial institutions) whose share of the market for a specific commodity exceeds thirty five per cent or which dominate a specific commodity market (hereinafter referred to as the "antimonopoly register").

Some transactions relating to shares (interest), assets of commercial entities and rights in respect of commercial entities are also subject to the prior consent of the antimonopoly body if the total assets of the transaction parties (their group of persons) exceeds 7 billion rubles or if the total proceeds of such parties (group of persons) exceeds 10 billion rubles, and if the total assets (according to the latest balance sheet) of an object of economic concentration and its group of persons exceeds two hundred and fifty million rubles or if one of the parties is listed in the antimonopoly register.

Special rules regulate transactions involving the shares (interest) and assets of financial institutions, and rights related to financial institutions and transactions, parties to which are members of the same group of persons.

Consequences of a Breach of the Antimonopoly Law

The antimonopoly body applies fairly severe measures in the event of a breach of the Competition Law: administrative penalties, including fines, mandatory liquidation or reorganization of entities and the declaration of the respective transactions as null and void.

In order to prevent breaches of the antimonopoly law, the antimonopoly body serves a written warning on the inadmissibility of actions which may entail a breach of the antimonopoly law.

In order to suppress actions (omissions) which will or may lead to inadmissibility, restriction or elimination of competition, the antimonopoly body shall issue a written warning to a dominating business entity demanding that it discontinue actions (omissions) bearing the signs of a breach of the antimonopoly law, eliminate the grounds and conditions causing the breach to occur and take steps to remedy the consequences of the breach. The antimonopoly body may not initiate proceedings on breach of the antimonopoly law without issuing a warning and before the expiration of period within which the demands specified therein are to be met.

The antimonopoly body is obliged to maintain a register of persons held administratively liable for breach of the antimonopoly law (the data contained therein shall not be published in the mass media or posted on the Internet).

Russia in the World Trade Organization

* by Vladimir Kilinkarov, Artur Osipov, Karina Starikova

Russia's Accession to the WTO

As of May 2015, 156 internationally-recognized states and customs territories were members of the WTO, including a number of the CIS countries. Approximately 30 countries are in negotiations to join the WTO.

One of the main conditions associated with the accession of a new member state is the alignment of its national legislation and foreign trade practices with WTO regulations.

Russia started negotiating its accession to the WTO in 1993. The final impediment to Russia's WTO entry was Georgia, which had been blocking its membership since the 2008 conflict. The parties argued about border controls for Abkhazia and South Ossetia, breakaway republics which had declared independence from Georgia. By the end of 2011 Russia and Georgia, with Switzerland mediating talks between the two, had reached an agreement on terms, and on 9 November the parties, with Switzerland acting as mediator, signed the agreement on Russia's WTO entry in Geneva. This was the last bilateral agreement on Russia's way to the WTO.

Upon Russia's WTO entry, members of the Working Group on Russia's WTO Accession indicated that Russia would have to submit information on its existing and planned free trade agreements, customs unions and economic union agreements for consideration by the WTO's Committee on Regional Trade Agreements (CRTA). Russia's representative confirmed in response to this that as to Russia's participation in preferential trade agreements, the provisions of the WTO Agreements would be observed, including Article XXIV of GATT 1994 and Article V of GATS, irrespective of whether such agreements were in effect on the date of accession or would come into force at a later date, and that Russia would, from the moment of its accession, ensure compliance with these WTO Agreements in terms of disclosures, consultations and other requirements with regard to the free trade zones and customs unions of which Russia is a member. He confirmed that after joining the WTO the Russian Federation would regularly make disclosures and submit copies of its free trade agreements to the CRTA.

On 16 December 2011 a set of documents for admitting Russia to the WTO was approved at the 8th WTO Ministerial Conference in Geneva. The set of documents includes the Working Group report describing Russia's trade regime and system-wide commitments, which confirm the compliance of this regime to WTO's standards, the Schedule of Tariff Concessions and the Schedule of Specific Commitments in Services. On 10 July 2012 the Russian State Duma adopted Federal Law No. 126-FZ "On Ratifying the Protocol on Accession of the Russian Federation to the Marrakesh Agreement Establishing the World Trade Organization of 15 April 1994" of 21 July, 2012.

Effects of Russia's Accession to the WTO

With regard to the legal effects of Russia's accession to the WTO, it should be noted that global practice currently defines **several ways of bringing national legislation into line with WTO legal regulations**.

Fundamental WTO documents can be translated into the national language and published as national laws (as happened in Brazil, for example).

The country can also recognize WTO agreements and, in cases when discrepancies occur, WTO legal regulations prevail over national laws (an approach adopted in Japan).

There is also the opposite approach. Section 102(a)(1) of the Uruguay Round Agreements Act, which establishes the connection between the WTO Agreements and US law, sets out that "no provision of any of the Uruguay Round Agreements, nor the application of any such provision to any person or circumstance that is inconsistent with any law of the United States shall have effect".

Russia has found its own way and **has decided to make national laws which would include the WTO regulations, sometimes verbatim**. It has turned out to be an extremely difficult process, since many WTO provisions often lose their legal significance when translated into Russian. The point is that all WTO legal regulations have emerged historically, and why they emerged, how they developed and how they grew into what they are now defines their very essence. That is why many of these regulations, when integrated into national laws, can only be correctly understood and transferred if legislators are aware of why and how these regulations emerged and developed and what meaning they ultimately acquired as a result of the interpretation of a particular term by numerous WTO bodies in the course of their work.

Legislators working on new foreign trade laws that comply with WTO rules have to take into account another peculiarity of Russia's legislative practice. Article 15 of the Constitution of the Russian Federation says that the provisions of an international agreement prevail over the provisions of national laws. That is why after Russia's WTO entry, WTO regulations will be directly included in Russia's legal system. This in turn will provoke **the emergence of a sui generis two-tier legal system in foreign trade** where national regulations disagree with WTO regulations.

Russia's accession to the WTO impels that all fundamental WTO **principles and rules** become applicable, including the following:

- mutual most-favored-nation treatment;
- mutual national treatment of foreign commodities and services;
- using mainly tariff methods of trade regulation;
- abandoning quantitative and other limitations;
- transparency of trade policies;
- resolving trade disputes through consultations, negotiations, etc.

From the economic perspective the main effect of Russia's accession to the WTO should be the liberalization and improvement of the business climate. It will help Russia diversify its economy and reduce its dependence on volatile oil prices. Russia's economy will become more competitive.

That is why Russia's WTO entry is an important event with long-range effects such as the gradual positive recognition of the Russian economy by foreign investors and the growth of competition. This in turn serves to enhance international investors' confidence in the Russian market and have positive effects on the economy as a whole and the banking sector in particular. In the short run it will help stop the outflow of capital, which is one of the major risk factors threatening Russia's banking industry according to IMF experts.

Thanks to Russia's accession to the WTO, Russian companies will be able to enter world markets.
The most intense competition will be in the mechanical engineering,

chemical, and pharmaceutical industries. Iron and steel companies will gain the most, while computer manufacturers and OEMs will be in a losing position. Due to only a slight decrease in import duties, profits from export sales will fall, though Russian companies will be able to gain a larger share of the domestic market thanks to the appreciation of the ruble.

Construction companies also favor Russia's membership of the WTO since it will have significant effects on the development of the construction market. These effects will be mainly positive. The most positive effects will include reducing the housing shortage, since the domestic construction sector alone cannot meet the annual demand for 80 million square meters of accommodation. In addition, the construction industry will get a kick-start in the regions of Russia, especially where housing development is traditionally slow, including Siberia and the Far East.

Increasing competition from foreign construction companies will stimulate the recovery of the market and help eliminate ineffective companies which offer no advantages either to the government or to the consumer. New technologies coming into Russia from abroad will also have a beneficial effect on the construction industry. The price per square meter is likely to decrease eventually, making middle-class private housing affordable. Mortgage options will also get an additional kick-start, which will increase the demand for residential property.

In the event that any member state commits unlawful acts against Russia, Russia will be able to file a complaint with the WTO's Dispute Settlement Body. The decisions of this body are binding at national level for every WTO member state. Only WTO member states represented by their governments are entitled to apply to this court. According to the "Government of the Russian Federation" federal constitutional law, the government takes measures to protect the interests of domestic manufacturers, contractors and service providers. Therefore, as a result of Russia's accession to the WTO the Russian government had legal options to protect domestic manufacturers—whatever is meant by this—in the international arena and in accordance with WTO regulations. This is perhaps the most important advantage of WTO membership, since the business sector obtained new legal remedies to protect its competitiveness.

WTO membership also required Russia to adapt **law enforcement practice in the field of customs valuation** to WTO regulations, which is definitely a positive aspect. Thus, there is no clear indication in Russian law as to whether or not credit interest should be included in the customs value of goods, while the WTO has addressed this issue (see Decision 3.1 of 1 October 1984 by the WTO Customs Valuation Committee, as amended on 12 May 1995).

Therefore, WTO laws and regulations contain solutions that are not easy to find in Russian law, which is why Russia's WTO entry will help promptly solve certain problems connected with foreign trade.

Effects of Russia's WTO entry for the Consumer

It is proposed that Russia's WTO entry will have the following effects on customs duties (and as a result, on the final product price):

- Duty rates for **imported drugs** will be reduced from 15–5 % to 6.5–5 % within the transition period, while duties for medical equipment and drug substances at the same time will fall even faster (up to 2–3 %).
- Russia's accession to the WTO will mostly have little or no effect on the **chemical market**. On the whole, duty rates will be reduced from 10% to 6.5–5 %. In cases where the decrease is more considerable, such as for cosmetics, soaps and detergents, linoleum and some plastic goods, the transition will take from 5 to 6 years.
- Duty rates for **processing, building, scientific and metering equipment** will be significantly reduced or canceled.
- Customs duties for **computers, their means of production and hardware components** will be canceled within 3 years after the accession. Customs duties for **consumer electronics** and appliances will be reduced from 15 % to 7–9 %.
- As for **vehicles**, customs tariffs at the moment of accession should be reduced to the level before the crisis, that is to 2009 tariffs. Customs duties for **new automobiles** will fall from 25 % to 15 % within 7 years. This will mainly occur within the next 3 years, which will, on the one hand, protect the interests of Russian buyers and consumers, and, on the other hand, allow for the implementation of major investment projects in automobile manufacturing involving foreign capital. At the same time, customs duties for **used cars** (pre-owned for 3 to 7 years) will be 20 %, having decreased from 25 % within the transition period.
- Customs duties for **ready-to-eat fish products** will decrease only slightly, from 15 % to 12.5–12 % within 1 to 3 years. As for raw fish, customs duties will be reduced for many types of this raw material from the current 10 % to 6–8 %, and even to 3–5 % in some cases.

- Customs duties for **milk, cream powder and concentrated cream and butter** will fall from 25 % to 20 %, thus bringing the rates back to the level before 1 January 2010. At the moment of accession the current tariff rate for tea and coffee will remain at the same level.
- Russia will reduce tariffs on some kinds of **animal foodstuffs** and pet food, including soy beans, mill cake and oil meal; fruit, vegetables and nuts which do not grow in Russia, such as pistachio nuts, peanuts, oranges, grapes, and bananas, especially on fruit and vegetables in the winter period. Import of **deficient raw materials for the food industry**, such as lactoserum, will become easier.
- Russia continues applying tariff quotas for **beef, pork and poultry** from the moment of its accession to the WTO. The term of the tariff quota regime for these kinds of meat is undefined. The tariff quota regime for pork will end on 31 December 2019. Access to the beef market will be the same, while for poultry and pork it will become more difficult.

According to the Working Group report, the average import tariff will be reduced from the current 10 % (as at June 2011) to 7.8 %. Russian chief negotiator Maxim Medvedkov commented at the WTO talks that tariffs would fall to the mid-2007 level, which means that Russia plans to reduce the so-called "anti-crisis" import duties. According to the Working Group report, the most sensitive industries such as the automotive industry and agriculture are successfully protected, and the transition period for these industries will be 7 and 8 years respectively.

In addition, upon the accession to the WTO Russia made commitments in more than 2/3 of service sectors included in the WTO classification. However, the commitments do not require changes in the current regulation system in most cases. The major exception to this rule is the insurance sector, where the total foreign participation quota for the sector should increase from 25 to 50%, while the 49 % limitation on foreign participation in individual companies in fields such as life insurance and mandatory insurance will increase to 51 % on the date of accession and will be canceled in 5 years. At the same time, starting from 2004, the 49 % limitation on foreign participation does not apply to life insurance and mandatory insurance companies if the capital comes from EU countries.

Nine years after Russia's accession to the WTO the so-called direct branches of foreign insurance companies will be allowed into the country. However, based on the limitations imposed by Russia's commitments, Russia will be able to introduce rules for entering the market similar to the rules for establishing legal entities, and create a similar business environment, which will significantly restrict their competitive advantages over Russian companies.

Certain changes also concern the education sector. Russia's accession to the WTO enables foreign universities to open branches in Russia.

Commitments in a number of sectors allow for the introduction of tougher measures compared with the existing regime. Thus, the Russian government will be able to impose a monopoly on wholesale alcohol distribution, if required. Russia's WTO entry also helps to increase in competition and reduce import prices, which will eventually provide benefit to Russian consumers and stimulate the modernization of manufacturing industry. Accession to the WTO will continue improving the functioning of different Russian institutions, particularly in fields such as customs regulation and public procurement. More transparent investment rules and trade dispute procedures should attract investment in the medium term.

According to the estimates of the World Bank, Russia's accession to the WTO will stimulate GDP growth by approximately 2.8 % in the short term, by 3.3 % in the medium term and by 11 % in the long term. At the same time, WTO membership should significantly help combat inflation with increased competition and direct reduction of import tariffs. Both these factors should have a positive effect for investors to reappraise the Russian securities market.

Contract Law Issues

* by Vladimir Kilinkarov, Natalia Zelentsova, Alina Kozmina

A contract is a universal instrument of commercial relations. In this regard, any foreigner wishing to do business in Russia should be aware of the main statutory provisions relating to contract law.

Under Russian law a **contract** is an agreement between two or more parties that establishes, modifies, or terminates private rights and obligations. As opposed to countries that use the Anglo-Saxon legal system, in Russian system contract provisions in Russia are mainly stipulated by law, in particular by the Civil Code of the Russian Federation in four parts. General rules on contracts are established in Part 1 of the Civil Code (1994, as amended), and certain types of contracts are stipulated in Part 2 of the Civil Code (1996, as amended).

The main principle on which Russian contract law is based is **freedom of contract**, i.e. any person may enter into any contract that is stipulated or not expressly provided for by law. Agreements that include elements of different contracts specified by law (so-called mixed contracts) are also possible. Moreover, the parties may determine any terms and conditions in the contract by their own choice, except in cases where the substance of certain contracts is specified by law. However, most of the legal regulations contained in the Civil Code are non-mandatory, and the parties to the contract may exclude some conditions specified in such legal regulations, or may alter the substance of these conditions.

General principle of good faith is another important principle of Russian contract law. Russian law also knows the presumption of good faith of participants of civil law relations.

Formation of a contract

A. The Civil Code contains general rules of contract formation. To enter into a contract, a **person or a legal entity must be legally capable.**

(1) Individuals have general legal capacity after the age of eighteen (but if a minor under eighteen years of age is married, he or she has full capacity to conclude a contract). The legal capacity of insane persons and persons addicted to alcohol or drugs can be annulled or limited by the decision of a court. Children between the ages of fourteen and eighteen have limited capacity to conclude a contract independently, but they may enter into any contracts by their own actions with the written approval of their parents or other legal representatives. A child under fourteen years of age may conclude inessential everyday transactions and dispose of funds with the consent of his/her parents or of any third parties.

(2) The capacity of legal entities to enter into a contract originates from the moment of their state registration and is terminated upon liquidation procedures. If a particular type of activity requires a license or permit, the legal entity obtains legal capacity to undertake such activity and form a contract on receipt of the special license or permit. Corporations and other legal entities may have **general** or **special legal capacity**. Special capacity restricts the scope of contracts permitted to the entity. Commercial legal entities normally have general legal capacity to conclude a contract, unless limited capacity is provided for by law or in the charter documents of certain types of entities. In general, a contract on behalf of a legal entity can be formed by their officers, acting in accordance with constituent documents and legal regulations.

B. In order to form a contract the parties **must agree on all substantial terms of the contract** in the required form. The substantial terms of a contract are its subject matter and also other terms which are described by the law as substantial or are required for contracts of a certain type.

A contract is deemed to have been formed at the time when the person who has made an offer receives full and unconditional acceptance. A conditional or partial acceptance is deemed to be a counter-offer and is not sufficient to form a contract. For certain types of contracts the law requires not merely consent to the terms of the contract in the required form, but also the physical transfer of a property into the possession of another party. In such a case, the contract is formed at the time of the transfer. A contract that requires mandatory state registration becomes effective after registration, unless otherwise stipulated by law.

An offer sets out the required details of the proposed contract and expresses the intention of the offeror to enter into contract with the person who accepts the offer on the terms provided therein. An offer must specify the substantial terms of the contract. An offer binds an offeror from the time the offeree receives the offer.

An offeror may revoke his offer by notifying the offeree before the latter receives the offer. An offer which has been received by an offeree may not be revoked during the period of time specified in it, or during the reasonable time required for its receipt and for communication of its acceptance to the offeror.

An advertisement or other general notification addressed to an indefinite number of persons not known to the offeror is deemed to be an invitation to make offers and is not an offer in itself, unless the advertisement/notification expressly states otherwise. An offer which includes all the essential terms of the future contract and the intention of the offeror to enter into contract under such terms with any person that accepts it is a public offer.

Acceptance means expressing one's consent to accept the offer and to enter into a contract. It should be noted that silence, i.e. failure to take action or make a statement on the basis of an offer, is normally not treated as acceptance. The law or customs, parties' agreement or usual course of business may override this default rule. Acceptance may also be expressed by rendering a performance (such as a transfer of funds or provision of services), which eliminates the need of a formal notice of acceptance. An acceptance may be revoked by a notice of revocation, which must be received by the offeror prior to or simultaneously with the notice of acceptance.

If a written offer does not specify a deadline for acceptance, a contract is deemed to have been formed if the acceptance is received within the timeframe specified by law or, if the law is silent on the matter, within the time normally required for acceptance. When a verbal offer is made without specifying a period for acceptance, a contract shall be deemed to have been formed only if the offeree accepts it immediately.

From June 1, 2015 a legal norm familiar to many legal systems is introduced to the Civil Code: protection from **unfair practice in the course of negotiations** on entering into a contract. Neither individuals nor legal entities shall be liable for failure to reach a contract in the course of negotiations. However, if either party conducts or terminates negotiations unfairly, it shall be liable to reimburse the other party for the losses incurred (expenses incurred in connection with conducting negotiations, loss of opportunity to enter into a contract with third party).

Unfair conduct may include, for example, conducting negotiations knowingly without intention to reach agreement, misrepresentation in respect of the proposed terms and conditions of the contract, unreasonable termination of the negotiations without prior notice to the other party.

The affected party shall be entitled to claim damages in the event of the disclosure or improper use of confidential information received by the other party in the course of the negotiations, regardless of whether or not the contract is concluded.

From June 1, 2015 a new concept of "**representation on the circumstances**" is also introduced. If, in the course of conclusion of a contract or thereafter, a party makes a misrepresentation in respect of circumstances that are material to the conclusion, performance or termination of the contract (including, *inter alia*, those related to the subject matter of the contract, its compliance with the applicable law, the availability of the necessary licenses and approvals, its financial position), it shall be liable to compensate losses incurred by the other party caused by unreliability of such representations, or to pay the penalty provided in the contract at the other party's request. Moreover, if the contract is deemed non-concluded or void, it shall not impede the reimbursement of losses or penalty recovery. The foregoing liability arises if the party which made the misrepresentations believed or reasonably believed that the other party would rely upon them.

C. **Form of Contracts**. Contracts may be concluded in verbal or written form. Verbal contracts are permitted if the law does not specifically prescribe another form. A contract that can be formed verbally is also deemed to be have been formed by conclusive actions. All contracts that are performed at the moment of their formation can be made verbally unless otherwise agreed by the parties or otherwise required by law.

A written form is required (i) for all contracts that include at least one legal entity as a party, (ii) for contracts between individuals for a value of over ten minimal statutory monthly wages and (iii) in other cases prescribed by law, irrespective of the amount.

It should be noted that according to the Civil Code as amended the requirement related to the mandatory written form of foreign trade transactions is cancelled – the form of such transactions is now subject to the general rules of the Civil Code.

Under Russian law, non-compliance with a written form of a contract normally entails the impossibility of relying on witness testimony as a means of proving the contract as well as its terms and conditions, but not the invalidity of a contract. In such a situation the contract may be proven by other evidence. In cases specifically provided for by law or agreed between the parties, non-compliance with the written form renders the contract null and void.

For some contracts mentioned by the law, certification by a notary (notarial form) is required. It is also required in cases when the parties have reached an agreement about notary form of the contract. The contract shall be null and void if such certification is not obtained. Compliance with a special procedure of state registration of contract is another condition of validity for certain contracts. In particular, state registration is required for some contracts involving title to land or other real estate objects, including some lease contracts (see *Real Estate and Construction* section).

D. It should be noted, that in the same way as a transaction, a contract may be deemed **invalid** on grounds set out in the RF Civil Code by virtue of its being adjudged invalid by a court (voidable transaction) or irrespective of such an adjudication (void transaction). A party to a transaction or other person as may be provided for by law may claim invalidation of a voidable transaction or enforcement of consequences of invalidity of a void transaction. In addition to a party to the transaction, a person that has a legally protected interest to invalidate the transaction can also claim for enforcement of consequences of invalidity of such transaction. Thus, persons who have no legal interest are not able to file the mentioned claims to a court. If a contract is adjudged void, the court's function is usually limited merely to the enforcement of the legal consequences provided for in the legislation. It should be taken into account that an invalid contract does not entail legal consequences except for those related to its invalidity and is invalid from the time of its conclusion. A court is entitled to refrain from the enforcement of the implications of invalidated transactions if their enforcement contravenes fundamental principles of public order and morality.

General rules in respect of the invalidity of transactions are listed in Part I of RF Civil Code. If a contract is invalid, each of the parties thereto undertakes to return to the other party all articles received pursuant to the contract, and if it is impossible to return such articles in kind, it undertakes to compensate their value in monies, unless other circumstances are provided for by law.

The law contains an exhaustive list of grounds on which transactions may be deemed invalid.

A few of them are listed below.

The following transactions are or may be held invalid:

- transactions that are not in compliance with the law or other legal acts;
- transactions concluded with breach of mandatory form requirements;
- transactions concluded with breach of mandatory state registration requirements;
- transactions concluded for a purpose deliberately inconsistent with the fundamental principles of law or morality;
- sham transactions (transactions concluded merely pro forma, without intention of entailing the relevant legal effect) and simulated contracts (contracts entered into in order to conceal another transaction);
- transactions concluded by a legal entity for the purposes of activity that is expressly restricted in its foundation documents (transactions contrary to objectives of company's activities;
- transactions concluded by a minor or by a citizen considered legally incapable or incapable of understanding his/her actions or controlling them;
- transactions concluded under the influence of error, deception, violation, menace or malice between a representative of one party and the other party, or in adverse circumstances;
- transactions concluded without necessary consent of a third party, corporate body or governmental authority;
- transactions concluded by a representative on behalf of a person being represented for his/her own benefit;
- transactions conducted by a representative, branch of a legal entity or a corporate body beyond the scope of its authority, as well as those conducted by the said persons that prejudice the interests of the represented person;
- transactions aimed at the disposal of property when such disposal is either prohibited or restricted by law (if the property is sequestered or if bankruptcy regulations apply).

There is a tendency of easing-off the legislators' approach to consequences of invalidation of transactions. Transactions which violate the law are now considered voidable, but not void, except for transactions that breach the public interest or rights of third parties.

Thus, such transactions create legal consequences until they are declared void by a court's decision. Therewith, legal consequences of transactions concluded for purposes contrary to the principles of public order and morality have become less strict: now collection of all proceeds from such transaction to the public revenues is applied only in cases where both parties to a transaction acted deliberately.

A party to a transaction should not behave in a contradictory way when demanding to declare such transaction void. Firstly, a party that confirmed the validity of a transaction by its behavior shall have no right to claim for declaring the transaction void on the grounds, which the party was or should have been aware of behaving in such a way. Secondly, if a person referring to the invalidity of a transaction is acting in bad faith, invalidating claims filed by such person shall have no legal value. The rule refers to cases where behavior of a person encouraged other persons to rely on the validity of the transaction after the transaction has been concluded. In addition, the party which received the performance from the counterparty under the B2B contract while completely or partially failed to fulfill its own obligations, as a general rule does not have the right to demand recognition of the contract null and void. These rules reflect the general principle of good faith of participants of civil relations.

It should be noted that a contract may be considered invalid only partially, in which case the invalid part of the contract does not influence the validity of the other parts thereof if it is possible to assume that the contract was concluded without the invalid part.

Performance of a contract

The Parties shall perform their contractual obligations with due diligence and in accordance with the terms and conditions of the contracts, rules of law and regulations, and, in the absence of such terms and conditions, rules or regulations, in accordance with the customs and/ or other normal standards of action. A creditor is entitled not to accept partial performance unless the parties specifically agree otherwise or performance in part is allowed by customs or by the rules of law.

The performance of a contract is incumbent upon the creditor under the contract or to a person designated by the creditor. A party rendering performance must verify that he is offering the performance to the proper person. In other words, a debtor bears the risk of rendering performance to an improper person. An obligor may commit any third party to render performance to a creditor, unless the obligation is such as to require performance in person. The beneficiary has to accept proper performance rendered by a third party in the following cases:

1) the debtor failed to perform a monetary obligation;
2) the third party is in danger of losing his/her right to property of the debtor as a result of beneficiary seeking enforcement against this property.

The period for performance may be fixed in the contract as the date or period of time when the performance must be rendered. If a contract does not contain a reference to a particular date or period of time as well as in cases when the period of performance of the obligation is determined by the moment of demand, the obligation should be performed within seven days after request of performance made by the obligee, unless the law, rules, regulations, customs or terms and conditions of the contract provide otherwise. From June 1, 2015 as a general rule the obligor is entitled to demand the obligee to accept performance if the latter files no claim on fulfillment of such obligation within a reasonable time period.

The law generally prohibits the unilateral repudiation or modification of a contract, but provides for certain cases when this is admissible by the law (such as a serious breach by the other party). The parties to a B2B contract are entitled to agree upon additional grounds that justify the unilateral repudiation or alteration of their obligations while in a B2C contract the right to modify or repudiate the contract unilaterally may be granted only to a consumer. This right may be subject to payment of a specific sum of money to the other party to contract from June 1, 2015.

The parties to a contract may agree on any place for the performance of the contract, unless a specific place is prescribed by law.

Contract remedies

The general remedy for failure to perform a contract is **compensation for damages**. In Russian law damages include direct losses (real damages, i.e. expenses incurred and/or to be incurred as a result of the breach, deterioration or loss of property) and lost profits (consequential damages). The person whose rights are infringed is entitled to recover as "special damages" all income realized by the debtor as a result of the breach. Compensation for damages caused by improper performance does not release the party in breach from rendering a performance that is still outstanding. However, by paying damages to a creditor for a failure to perform, the party in breach is released from rendering performance. From June 1, 2015 the RF Civil Code introduces the rule according to which full compensation for damages shall imply that as a result of such compensation the creditor shall be in the same position as it would have been if the obligation had been duly performed. In addition, unless otherwise set out by law, if the creditor applied other remedies for its breached rights provided either by law or by the contract, it shall not be deprived of its right to claim from the debtor compensation for damages caused by the non-performance or improper performance of the obligation. This rule also comes into force on 1 June, 2015.

Damages may be compensated upon the termination of the contract. From June 1, 2015 the RF Civil Code introduces the rule according to which in the event that the non-performance or improper performance of the contract by the debtor entails its early termination and the creditor enters into another transaction instead (substitute transaction), he/she shall be entitled to claim from the debtor compensation for damages in the form of the difference between the price fixed in the terminated contract and that of the comparable goods, works or services under the substitute transaction. If the creditor does not enter into a substitute transaction, but in respect of the performance under the terminated contract there is an available current price for the comparable goods, works or services, the creditor shall be entitled to claim from the debtor compensation for damages in the form of the difference between the price fixed in the terminated contract and the current price. Thus, the RF Civil Code provides for recovery of not only specific, but also abstract damages.

Penalties are another common remedy that applies if provided for by law or in a contract. Penalties do not necessarily prevent compensation of damages. The default rule is that where a penalty is payable for breach of contract, any losses may be recovered only in the part that exceeds the amount of penalty (set-off penalty). However, a punitive penalty (recoverable on top of damages), an alternative penalty (where the creditor has an option to recover either penalty or losses) and a liquidated penalty (only the penalty but not losses are paid in case of the breach) are legal as well. A penalty may be expressed as a fixed amount or as a percentage of the value of the obligation. It may also be linked to the duration of the delay. The court has discretion to reduce the amount of a penalty that is disproportionate to the damage caused by a breach. From June 1, 2015 contractual penalties payable by a person conducting entrepreneurial activity may be reduced only if the creditor gains unjustified benefits from such penalties.

If a party defaults on a contractual obligation to provide a particular item or to render work or a service, the other party may entrust **performance of the obligation** to a third party or to perform it itself, and after that recover costs and damages from the party in default.

Special liability is provided by the law for the violation of a monetary obligation. If a person fails to return or pay money under a contract, the other party is entitled to recover interest accrued on the amount during the period of default. From June 1, 2015 the interest rate on obligations expressed in rubles is defined by reference to the average bank interest rates on deposits of individuals published by the Central Bank of Russia which were established during the relevant period. If the amount of damages caused by the breach of a monetary obligation exceeds the amount of interest, the creditor is entitled to compensation of damages for the part that exceeds this amount. An obligation may provide for a different interest rate or other rules of interest and damages. The contractual penalties and the foregoing interest for breach of the financial obligation can't be charged at the same time unless otherwise is provided by law or a contract. Similarly to the rule related to the reduction of penalties, the amount of the foregoing interest may also be reduced in the event that it is disproportionate to the consequences of the breach of the obligation (the rules are applicable from 1 June, 2015).

As opposed to Anglo-Saxon legal system countries, **specific performance** is one of the main remedy in Russian system. For instance, the creditor may demand seizure and transfer to its possession of a designated item that was to be given to him/her under the contract. To award a remedy the court establishes all conditions of liability, such as: infringement of civil law, unfavorable consequences to the rights of third parties caused by the infringement and, in certain cases, the fault of an offender. An element of fault is found where an offender has acted deliberately or negligently. Unlike in criminal prosecutions, guilt is presumed in civil cases. To be exonerated from liability, an offender has to prove that he was not guilty of the breach.

In cases where both the injured party and the offender are at fault, comparative fault rules apply and the degree (amount) of liability is adjusted accordingly. Liability for breach of an obligation in the course of entrepreneurial activity arises even where no fault at all exists on part of an offender. Entrepreneurs are absolved from liability only where the breach is caused by force-majeure.

From 1 June, 2015 the RF Civil Code provides for the parties to a B2B contract can set out in the contract an obligation of one party to compensate the proprietary losses of another party that arise in connection with oncoming of certain circumstances indicated in the contract, but not related to its breach by any of the parties.

These losses may be caused by failure to perform the obligation or by filing claims against the creditor by third parties. Such losses may be compensated only in the amount provided by the contract.

For certain categories of transactions the law provides for **limited liability**. A clause on limitation of liability may also be included in the contract.

Amendment and Termination of Contracts

Amendment or termination of a contract is possible only by agreement between the parties, unless otherwise is stipulated by law. On the demand of one of the parties the contract may be amended or terminated by the decision of a court in the case of an essential violation of the contract by the other party. An essential violation is deemed to be a violation of the contract by one of the parties that entails losses for the other party, depriving that party to a considerable extent it of what it could have counted upon when concluding the contract.

Another ground for the amendment or cancellation of a contract is an essential change of circumstances undergone by the parties since the conclusion of the contract. A change of circumstances is recognized as essential if they have changed to such an extent that, if the parties could have envisaged it, the contract would not have been concluded by them or would have been concluded on essentially different terms.

In the case of a unilateral refusal to perform a contract in full or in part, where such a refusal is permitted by law or by agreement between the parties, the contract may be accordingly regarded as terminated or amended.

Real Estate & Construction

* by Sergey Bakeshin, Evgeniy Druzhinin

Definition of Real Estate

There are two types of immovable objects in Russia:

• objects that are immovable by their nature;
• objects that are immovable by virtue of the law.

According to Clause 1 of Article 130 of the RF Civil Code the following objects are considered to be immovable (immovable property, real estate): plots of land, subsoil plots and everything that is inseparable from the land – in other words, objects that are impossible to move without causing incommensurate damage to their designated purpose, including buildings and objects of unfinished construction (immovable by their nature). The following objects are also regarded as being immovable: aircraft and sea vessels, inland vessels and space objects that are subject to state registration (immovable by virtue of the law). Other property may also be declared by law to be immovable objects.

A specific type of real estate is reclaimed territories (so-called "artificial land plot", "artificially created land plot") – mean constructions created from sea or riverbeds either by means of banking up or depositing of soil or using other technologies and recognized as plots of land after their commissioning. The procedure for creating these artificial plots of land is governed by the Federal Law "On Artificial Land Plots Created from Sea or Riverbeds under Federal Ownership and Amendment of Specific Legislative Acts of the Russian Federation" of 19 July 2011.

The concept of a "unified property complex" was introduced in RF Civil Code by Federal Law No. 142-FZ dated 2 July, 2013. A "unified property complex" means all the buildings, constructions or similar facilities either physically or technologically inseparably connected (including linear features – railways, electricity transmission lines, pipelines, etc.), or located on the same plot of land if consolidation of these facilities into one immovable property is reflected in the unified state register of rights to immovable property.

It should be noted that the Russian legislation has not accepted the concept of a "unified facility", according to which any object built on a land plot is not recognized as an independent immovable object, but is only an improvement of such a land plot. However, various articles of the Civil Code and the Land Code of the Russian Federation (hereinafter – the Land Code) establish the general principle of the unity of the fate of the land plot and immovable objects situated on it, which, however, has a number of exceptions.

Real Estate Rights

In Russia rights to real estate are traditionally divided into rights in rem and rights of obligation. The following rights are considered to be rights in rem: right of ownership, right of economic management, right of operational management, right of lifetime inheritable possession, right of permanent (indefinite) use, easements. The following rights are considered as rights of obligation: leasing rights, right of free use for a definite period, mortgages.

Right of ownership means the legally secured possibility to possess, use and dispose of property at the owner's discretion for the owner's benefit by means of conducting in respect of such property any actions that do not conflict with the law and do not breach the rights and legally protected interests of other persons, and also the possibility to eliminate interference by third persons in the said sphere of possession, use and disposal. In accordance with Clause 2 of Article 8 of the RF Constitution, private, state, municipal and other types of property are equally recognized and protected in Russia. Private property is divided into the personal property of citizens and the property of legal entities; state property is divided into federal property (owned by the Russian Federation) and property belonging to constituent territories of the Russian Federation (republics, territories, regions, cities with federal status, autonomous regions and autonomous districts). Urban and rural settlements and other municipalities act as subjects of municipal property.

Rights of economic management and operational management are specific types of rights in rem. They are the rights of legal entities to the use of the owner's property, aimed at establishing a property basis for the independent participation of legal entities that are not owners in civil rights matters. Only legal entities may be subjects of the rights of economic management and operational management. Moreover, not all legal entities may be the subjects of such rights, but only enterprises and institutions that have a specific legal form.

The difference between the right of economic management and the right of operational management is in the essence and scope of competence in respect of property granted by the owner to the right holders. The right of economic management belonging to a unitary enterprise is essentially much more wide-ranging than the right of operational management, which may be granted either to institutions or to state enterprises. The right of operational-management belonging to an autonomous institution, in its turn, is much more wide-ranging than the rights of a budgetary and private institution or a state enterprise.

Right of permanent (indefinite) use of a plot of land means the possession and use of a plot of land within the limits established by the law, other legislative acts and an act granting the plot of land for use. Plots of land may be granted for permanent (indefinite) use to state and municipal institutions, state enterprises, centers of the historical heritage of Presidents of the Russian Federation who have left office, as well as to governmental authorities and local authorities. Citizens may not be granted plots of land for permanent (indefinite) use since 30 October, 2001.

Right of lifetime inheritable possession is a right in rem stipulated in civil and land legislation. Only individuals may be subject to this law. The provision of plots from state and municipal lands on the basis of this right was terminated on 30 October 2001.

It should be noted that the right of lifetime inheritable possession as well as the right of permanent (indefinite) use (for persons who cannot be granted such a right in accordance with the current legislation) are to be renewed as property rights, and in some cases – as a rent. The term for such renewal – till 01 July, 2012 – is established exclusively for legal entities being neither state nor municipal unitary enterprises. Article 7.34 of the Code of Administrative Offences of the Russian Federation provides for the appropriate penalty for violation of renewal terms. The current legislation does not provide for other consequences of delay in renewal.

Easement means the right of restricted use. A private easement is established by agreement between its owner and other property users (most frequently land-tenants) in order to satisfy their interests, which may not be guaranteed without establishing an easement (for instance, a right of way across a plot of land, the laying of facilities *etc).*, and shall be registered in accordance with the procedure established for the registration of real estate rights. A public easement shall be established by law or other legal act of the Russian Federation, a regulation of a constituent territory of the Russian Federation or a regulation of local government if it is necessary to guarantee the interests of the state, local government or local population, without withdrawal of the plots of land. The easement accompanies the plot of land and may not be the subject of independent disposal by its user. Encumbrance of a plot of land by an easement does not deprive the owner of the rights of possession, use and disposal of the plot. An owner of a plot of land encumbered by an easement is entitled, unless otherwise provided for by law, to demand a commensurate payment for use of the plot of land from those for whose benefit the easement was established. Buildings and other real estate, limited use of which is necessary regardless of the use of the plot of land, may be encumbered by an easement.

Real estate lease means the granting of some property by its owner to another person for temporary possession or temporary use on a remuneration basis. The lessee is obliged to possess and use the leased property in accordance with the terms and conditions of the lease agreement and, if such terms and conditions are not specified in the agreement, he/she must possess and use the leased property in accordance with its designated purpose.

Free temporary property use means the temporary use of property by the borrower without the payment of remuneration to the lender. Only one restriction related to the structure of borrowers is stipulated by law: a commercial organization may not grant property for free use to its founder, participant, executive officer or member of its management or control bodies.

A **mortgage** is a pledge on real estate. Two kinds of mortgage are established by Russian Federation legislation: a mortgage by virtue of the law and a mortgage by virtue of an agreement (see below).

Acquisition of Real Estate Title

It is customary in Russia to distinguish between primary and derivative methods of property rights. Primary methods do not depend on the rights of the previous owner; in accordance with derivative methods a title may be transferred to a subsequent owner from his/her predecessor.

The following methods are the primary methods of acquiring real estate title: creation (construction or complete reconstruction) of a new object, unauthorized construction, acquisition of title to ownerless real estate and acquisitive prescription.

Succession is the main distinguishing mark of the derivative methods of acquisition of real estate title. They include: acquisition of real estate under agreements, as a legacy or as a result of the restructuring of a legal entity.

State Registration of Real Estate Rights and Transactions Therewith

The creation, transfer, restriction and termination of right of ownership and all other rights in rem to real estate in Russia take place in accordance with a specific procedure that requires observance of the written form of transaction and mandatory state registration of such legal facts.

In cases provided for by the law the transaction itself is subject to state registration. The following transactions currently require state registration: agreement on lease of a building or facility (premises therein) concluded for a term of not less than one year (par. 2, art. 651 of the RF Civil Code), agreement on lease or free temporary use of a plot of land concluded for a term of not less than one year (par. 2, art. 26 of the RF Land Code), agreement on lease of other types of immovable objects irrespective of their period (par. 2, art. 609 of the RF Civil Code), as well as real estate mortgage agreement (par. 1, art. 10 of the Federal Law dated 16.07.1998 № 102-FZ "On Mortgage") and shared construction participation agreement (par. 3, art. 4 of the Federal Law dated 30.12.2004. № 214-FZ "On Participation in the shared construction of apartment buildings and other immovable objects and on amendments to several legislative acts of the Russian Federation").

In accordance with par. 1, art. 164 of the RF Civil Code in cases when the law provides for state registration of transactions, the legal consequences of a transaction occur after its registration. A transaction involving changes to the conditions of the registered transaction is also subject to state registration.

State registration is carried out on the entire territory of the Russian Federation in accordance with a system of recording the rights established in respect of every real estate object. The corresponding records are entered in the Unified State Register of Real Estate Rights and Transactions Therewith, which contains information on the terminated and existing rights to real estate objects, information concerning these properties and the title-holders. Since state registration of real estate rights is public, the body carrying out state registration is obliged to provide any interested person with information about any object. State registration of rights shall be conducted within one month from the moment of submission of the application and the documents required for state registration in case a shorter period is not prescribed for such actions.

Since state registration is the only proof of the existence of a registered right, a registered right to real estate may be disputed only in court.

State registration of real estate rights and transactions therewith in Russia is regulated by a special law (see Federal Law No. 122-FZ "On the State Registration of Real Estate Rights and Transactions Therewith" of 21 July 1997).

Characteristics of the Purchase of Real Estate by Foreign Nationals

Foreign nationals may acquire title to or lease real estate, taking into account the restrictions imposed by the legislation of the Russian Federation.

On the whole, foreign nationals and legal entities enjoy a national regime in Russia and may acquire, own, use and dispose of real estate on the same terms as Russian individuals and legal entities. Any exceptions to this rule shall be expressly established by federal law.

Thus, in accordance with the RF Land Code, foreign nationals, stateless persons and foreign legal entities may not own plots of land in border territories. Foreign nationals may not be provided with plots of land owned by the state or a municipality free of charge. In addition, it is not permitted to transfer the right of ownership of agricultural lands. Such lands may be possessed and used only on a leasehold basis. As far as buildings and other structures are concerned, if they are not located in border territories and are not classified objects, no restrictions apply.

Construction in Russia

Construction (and complete reconstruction) is one of the primary methods of acquisition of the right to real estate. A construction object shall be considered as an object of real estate right only upon special procedures of commissioning, technical and cadastral registration. Prior to that, the newly constructed real estate does not exist in law. Moreover in most cases a construction object should pass state registration of rights (See **State Registration of Real Estate Rights and Transactions Therewith**) to enter civil circulation.

For state registration of a newly constructed object it is required to submit documents confirming the construction of the object and the rights to the plot of land on which it has been constructed (and documents confirming the rights to the object used as a basis for complete reconstruction if applicable). The owner of a plot of land shall obtain title to a building or other real estate constructed or created on that plot of land only subject to the observation of the requirements of the law and other legislative acts, including construction standards and rules.

Compliance with the relevant standards and rules shall be ensured at the following stages: a) the drafting of the design documents, b) the issuance of a construction permit, c) the issuance of a commissioning permit. In some cases provided by law construction work may be carried out without obtaining a construction permit and commissioning permit subsequently.

A construction permit is a document confirming compliance of the design documents with the development plan for a plot of land, granting the developer the right for the construction or reconstruction of capital construction objects. A commissioning permit is a document confirming the completion of the construction or reconstruction of a capital construction object.

An unauthorized construction means a real estate build on a plot of land not designated for these purposes, or a build without the necessary permits or in material breach of city planning and construction standards and rules. An unauthorized construction shall be demolished. However, in some cases a court may adjudicate that a person who owns the plot of land where such a construction was built has the title to the unauthorized construction.

The principal form of contract relating to construction in Russia is the construction contract stipulated by the RF Civil Code (see Clause 3 of Article 37 of the RF Civil Code). Under a construction contract a contractor undertakes to construct a specific object or carry out other construction works pursuant to the client's orders within the terms of the contract, and the client undertakes to create the conditions necessary for the contractor to carry out the work, accept the result of the work and pay the stipulated price.

One of the specific characteristics of the legal regulation of construction contract relations is the existence of a system of technical regulations governing the technical processes relating to the design of construction objects, the undertaking of erection, start-up and commissioning works, and the determination of technical requirements in respect of materials, structures and items used for the construction. The most important documents for technical regulation system are Technical Regulations which are to be adopted in the form of Federal Laws. Before adopting relevant Technical Regulations previous regulatory and technical documents are valid. First and foremost, these are the construction standards and regulations (SNiP) and sanitary standards and regulation (SanPiN). State and industry standards (GOST, OST) and technical specifications (TU) are also widely applied.

For major investment projects implemented under a construction contract, it is normal to employ several contractors to carry out the work. Relations between clients and contractors may take various legal forms, but the most common is the general contract system, under which a client enters into a contract with one person (the general contractor), who in turn engages other groups of persons (subcontractors) to carry out the contractual obligations. The subcontractors are entrepreneurs: organizations (construction, erection, commissioning and others) incorporated in various legal forms, and individual entrepreneurs.

In order to carry out work in the construction (as well as design and engineering survey) field an organization or individual entrepreneur should be a member of a self-regulating organization (SRO) in the construction field and have a certificate of competence relating to a specific type of work.

Sale and Purchase of Real Estate

The RF Civil Code is the basic legislation regulating the legal regime for the sale and purchase of real estate. The regulations of the RF Civil Code are expanded in codifying statutes and other federal laws of the Russian Federation.

The sale and purchase of real estate is the most common method of acquiring the right to ownership of real estate in Russia. Under a real estate sale and purchase agreement, the seller undertakes to transfer to the buyer the title to a plot of land, building, apartment or other real estate.

A real estate sale and purchase agreement shall be executed in writing by drawing up a single document to be signed by the parties thereto. It shall contain information precisely describing the transferred real estate and its price. According to the position of the Higher Arbitration Court for the individualization of the subject matter of the contract of sale of immovable property it is sufficient to indicate the cadastral number of real estate objects in the contract; nevertheless that does not exclude the possibility of individualization of the subject matter by specifying the other information in case of the absence of cadastral number (par. 2 of the Resolution of the Plenum the RF Higher Arbitration Court dated 11.07.2011 N 54 "On some issues of resolution of disputes arising from contracts on immovable property, which will be constructed or acquired in the future"). We should also note that only a land plot which passed the cadastral registration can be the subject of contract of sale (par. 1, art. 37 of the RF Land Code).

Contracts of sale of immovable property, which will be constructed or acquired by the seller in the future have recently become widespread. Relations between an investor and a developer can be also regulated by such a contract. The transfer of ownership right to the constructed property can be registered only after the registration of ownership right of the seller. Such contracts are expressly provided for by the RF Civil Code and are governed by the general rules applicable to contracts of sale of immovable property. We should note that in accordance with the current legislation it is unacceptable to conclude contracts of sale of apartments in apartment buildings which will be constructed or acquired by the seller in the future with individuals. Shared construction participation agreement is the main legal form for such relationships regulated by the Federal Law dated 30.12.2004 № 214-FZ "On Participation in the shared construction of apartment buildings and other immovable objects and on amendments to several legislative acts of the Russian Federation". Other legal forms for such relationships are exhaustively listed in par. 2 art. 1 of this Federal Law.

In a case where the seller is the owner of the plot of land on which the transferred building or other structure is situated, the right of ownership of the plot of land shall be transferred to the purchaser. The sale of property situated on a plot of land not owned by the seller is permitted without the prior consent of the owner of the plot, provided that it does not contradict the terms and conditions of use of the plot established by law or by agreement. In the event of the sale of such real estate, the buyer shall acquire the right to use the plot of land on the same conditions as the seller of the real estate.

Privatization of Real Estate

In accordance with RF legislation, privatization means the compensatory alienation of state property (property of the Russian Federation or constituent territories of the Russian Federation) or municipal property (property of municipalities) to the ownership of individuals and (or) legal entities. Privatization is based on the recognition of the equal rights of purchasers of state and municipal property and the transparency of the activities of state and local authorities. Not all types of state and municipal property may be privatized. Some categories of plots of land, natural resources and real estate belonging to state nature reserves may not be privatized.

The privatization of property in Russia is effected in accordance with the Federal Law "On the Privatization of State and Municipal Property" dated 21 December, 2001 except for the issues related to the provision of land plots for the purpose of construction and operation of real estate, and other special types of privatization.

The Government of the Russian Federation annually approves a forecast plan (program) of privatization of federal property for the year. The structure and price of privatized property shall be determined during privatization. In Russia privatization may be carried out by means of any of ten methods of privatization, subject to the observance of special characteristics of the privatization of certain types of property. The methods of privatization include: the transformation of a unitary enterprise into an open joint-stock company; the sale of state or municipal property at auction or tender; the sale of publicly owned shares of open joint-stock companies outside the RF; the sale of shares of open joint-stock companies through a trade organizer on the securities market; the sale of state or municipal property by means of a public offer or without announcing the price; the contribution of state or municipal property to the charter capitals of open joint-stock companies, and the sale of shares of open joint-stock companies based on the results of trust management.

The privatization process in Russia consists of several phases: 1) the filing of a privatization request; 2) the adoption of a resolution on the privatization of a specific object by the authorized state or local government body; 3) the drawing up and approval of the privatization plan; 4) the conclusion of an agreement with the purchaser of the privatized enterprise (property).

Privatization legislation stipulates demands on purchasers of privatized objects. State and municipal unitary enterprises, including state and municipal enterprises and other legal entities in whose charter capital the share of the Russian Federation, its constituent territories and municipalities exceeds 25%, may not act as purchasers. An exception is the contribution of state and municipal property to the charter capital of an open joint-stock company.

Provision of land plots being state or municipal property

In accordance with the art. 39.20 of the RF Land Code citizens and legal entities which have ownership rights in relation to buildings and facilities located at land plots have the exclusive right to purchase such land plots or to acquire the right of lease in relation to them.

The vast majority of land plots not occupied by buildings or facilities are state-owned. In accordance with par. 1, art. 16 of the RF Land Code land plots not owned by citizens, legal entities or municipalities belong to the state. Very often such property is not distinguished between the Russian Federation and its constituent territories (regions).

Pursuant to Federal Law No. 137-FZ "On Enactment of the Land Code of the Russian Federation" of 25 October 2001 those land plots, the public domain over which is not delimited, shall be, as a general rule, deposed by local government authorities. The said authorities also dispose of those land plots that are in municipal ownership. Exception is made for cities of federal importance (Moscow, St. Petersburg, Sevastopol), in which such deposal is carried out by executive bodies of the indicated constituent territories of the Russian Federation.

Also, from 05 July 2014 authorities to depose land plots can be delegated to the RF constituent territories according to law of the RF constituent territories.

As a general rule provision of land plots for construction is carried out by means of an auction. Full list of cases when land plots can be provided without a prior auction is defined in the RF Land Code. In the vast majority of cases the relationship related to provision of land plots for the purposes of construction are formalised by a lease agreement.

Lease of Real Estate

The main legislation regulating the lease of real estate is the RF Civil Code and the RF Land Code.

Under a lease agreement for a building or other structure, provided for by the RF Civil Code, the lessor undertakes to transfer to the lessee for remuneration temporary possession or temporary use of a building or other structure, or non-residential premises located in such a building or other structure, providing the lessee with the right to the part of the plot of land that is occupied by the real estate and essential for its use.

Land lease is similarly regulated by the RF Land Code. Lease of the other real estate objects is regulated by the general rules of the RF Civil Code.

A lease agreement for a building or other structure shall be executed in writing by drawing up a single document to be signed by the parties thereto. As a general rule other real estate lease contracts concluded for a period of more than a year, and if at least one of the parties to a contract is a legal person – then regardless of the period, must be concluded in writing. Traditionally, these contracts are also executed in writing by drawing up a single document to be signed by the parties thereto.

An agreement shall contain a provision on the agreed amount of rent – otherwise the agreement shall be deemed not to have been concluded. The right to the plot of land on which the leased property is situated and essential for its use shall be automatically transferred to the lessee.

Real Estate Pledges (Mortgages)

A mortgage is one of the ways of guaranteeing fulfillment of obligations in the Russian Federation. A mortgage is a real estate pledge and constitutes encumbrance of title to an object, restricting the possibility for the owner of disposing of the object.

The main regulations governing mortgages in Russia are the RF Civil Code, the RF Law "On Pledges" of 29 May 1992, the Federal Law "On Mortgages (Real Estate Pledges)" of 16 July 1998, the RF Housing Code, and Federal Law No. 122-FZ "On the State Registration of the Rights to Real Estate and Transactions Therewith" of 21 July 1997.

In the event of a property being mortgaged, it is not transferred to the mortgagee, but the rights of the mortgagor relating to the disposal of the mortgaged object may be exercised only with the prior consent of the mortgagee. A building or other construction may not be mortgaged without a simultaneous mortgage of the plot of land on which it is situated.

A mortgage is formalized by a mortgage agreement, which is to be executed in writing by drawing up a single document to be signed by the parties thereto and is subject to mandatory state registration. The establishment of a mortgage right may be accompanied by the issuance of a mortgage deed, which is a registered security.

Protection of Objects of Cultural Heritage

The legal regulation of relations connected with the protection of objects of cultural heritage is based on the RF Constitution, the RF Civil Code, the Basic Legislative Principles of the Russian Federation Related to Culture, the Federal Law "On Objects of Cultural Heritage (Historical and Cultural Monuments) of Peoples of the Russian Federation", as well as the laws of constituent territories of the Russian Federation relating to state protection of objects of cultural heritage within the scope of their authority.

Objects of cultural heritage include real estate with paintings, sculptures, works of decorative applied art, and objects and articles of material culture that originated as a result of historical events and are of value in terms of history, archeology, town planning, arts, science and technology, and are evidence of epochs and civilizations, genuine sources of information about the origin and development of culture.

Legal entities, citizens and their associations that use, manage or own objects of cultural heritage are obliged to take care of those objects of cultural heritage, observe the rules for their protection, use, registration and restoration established by the legislation of the Russian Federation.

Protection of objects of cultural heritage means a system of legal, organizational, financial, material and technical, informational and other measures aimed at revealing, registering and studying objects of cultural heritage, preventing their destruction or damage and controlling their preservation and use. This system includes state control over the observation of legislation relating to the protection and use of objects of cultural heritage, state registration of objects with marks of cultural heritage, the carrying-out of a historical and cultural examination, the imposition of liability for the damage, demolition or destruction of an object of cultural heritage, and the issuance of permission to undertake work to preserve an object of cultural heritage.

An owner of an object of cultural heritage undertakes to preserve it. Such obligations act as restrictions (encumbrances) of the property right to the object and shall be specified in a preservation order of the holder of title to an object of cultural heritage. Preservation order copy is an essential part of the agreement providing for transfer of ownership to an object of cultural heritage.

Preservation order is subject to the approval of the appropriate bodies for protection of objects of cultural heritage.

Preservation order should include requirements to the maintenance of the object of cultural heritage, conditions of providing access to it to citizens, the order and timing of the restoration, repair and other works for its preservation, as well as other requirements that ensure safety of the object.

If a decision is made to exclude an object of cultural heritage from the register, a preservation order in respect of that object becomes ineffective from the date the decision is made.

Public-Private Partnerships in Infrastructure

* by Vladimir Kilinkarov, Alina Kozmina

Brief information summary:

A public-private partnership as a form of implementation of projects in infrastructure provides for cooperation of public and private partners based on consolidation of investments and allocation of risks aimed to resolve public and socially important objectives carried out by means of implementation of investment projects related to the objects falling within public interest and being under public control. [1]

PPP (Public-Private Partnership) emerged in Great Brian in early 90-s of the 20th century in connection with implementation of a new public property management concept, namely a private financial initiative (PFI). Later on PPP was spread to Europe, USA, Australia, Canada and other countries. For 20 years of its existence PPP gained a reputation of an effective tool for cooperation between public and private enterprises in course of implementation of large socially important investment programs and projects in such areas as education, healthcare, road construction, nature management, housing and utility services, public transport, agriculture, forestry, electric energy industry, *etc.*

PPP is important since its application permits saving significant budgetary funds thanks to more efficient use of them and attracting private investments, introducing those innovations that private enterprises possess, decreasing in cost of public services for consumers, diverting state from being directly involved in production permitting it to focus on organisational and controlling functions.

The development of PPP in this meaning, in Russia usually referred to as a '*state*-private partnership' (sometimes considering that municipal projects fall outside the concept of PPP and too small

---

1   A.V. Belitskaya *Legal mechanism for implementation of public-private partnership in the social sphere //* Russian annual bulletin of entrepreneurial (commercial) law. No. 5, 2011 // Ed. by V.F. Popondupulo. SPb, 2012. P.197.

for PPP structuring), has just commenced in our country, however prospects for implementation of this institution for realization of large and medium-sized infrastructure projects on our vast territory suffering budget finance problems look more than encouraging.

In general, regulatory environment for public-private partnership in Russia is **rather inconsistent**, mostly due to the **lack of fundamental federal law regulating PPP**. Specifically, there is no definition of PPP facilitating understanding of the essence of this phenomenon, principles of its organisation and development and, consequently, systematization and unification of regulation of this institution.

In the absence of the unified law, the federal PPP regulation system is represented by a number of federal laws and subordinate legislation governing specific private and public legal relationships arising in course of implementation of PPP projects.

Federal Legislation

The fundamentals of public-private regulations and general provisions governing obligations covering all the types of PPP agreements lay in the **first and second parts of the Russian Civil Code**.

So articles 1, 421 of the Russian Civil Code enshrine the principle of freedom of agreement permitting generally to enter into PPP agreements, both provided by legislation and not, and to determine the terms of conditions of such agreement at own discretion, unless otherwise expressly provided by legislation.

At the same time parties are entitled to enter into mixed contracts containing elements of different agreements provided by law or other legal instruments (par. 3 article 421 of the Russian Civil Code). Relationship between the parties to a mixed contract are governed by respective parts of the rules on agreements (second part of the Russian Civil Code, for example, provisions on lease, contract, fee-based services, loans and credits, insurance, general partnership, *etc.*; as well as special legislation provisions), the elements of which can be found in a mixed contract, unless otherwise appear from the parties' agreement or the essence of such mixed contract. This provision allows to compensate the lack of special regulation of PPP obligations, and its applicability to concession agreements as to mixed contracts is underpinned by par. 2 article 3 of the Federal Law No. 1151-FZ "On Concession Agreements" of 27 July, 2005.

Despite the availability of the principle of freedom of contract in Russian law, PPP as one of the most resource-demanding forms of investment activity with a long payoff period requires special regulation, permitting to mitigate political and legal enforcement risks still more or less common for Russia. The special feature of the Russian legislation governing individual types of obligations, different elements of agreements, terms and conditions for their conclusion, performance and termination which in court practice and legal theory is often deemed as qualified discretion of lawmaker restricting freedom of parties to choose a type of agreement even taking into account that such general norms are not well adapted to the specific relationships of PPP parties, in addition to the peculiarities of regulation of deals concluded under conditions, instruments to secure obligations, restrictions of budget and tax legislations as well as state and municipal procurement legislation applicable to individual types of contractual obligations, the necessity of free allocation of risks and warranties - all these counts in favour of comprehensive regulation of PPP institution in the Russian context.

First attempts of such comprehensive regulation are reflected firstly in the **Federal Law No. 225-FZ "On Production Sharing Agreements" of 31 December, 1995** creating legal platform for relationships emerging in course of Russian and foreign investments in exploration, survey and extraction of raw materials within the jurisdiction of Russia based on production sharing agreements, and afterwards in the **Federal Law No. 115-FZ "On Concession Agreements" of 27 July, 2005** (below referred to as the "**Concession Law**") adopted ten years later. The latter became the most notable landmark in development of Russian regulation of PPPs, however in practice this law do not meet all expectations of the investor.

Concession Law

The Concession Law governs those relationships that arise in connection with preparing to, entering into, performance and termination of concession relationships under which one party (a concessionary, private partner) undertakes at his expense (i) to create and/or reconstruct property specified in such agreement (real property or real property and movable property technologically connected with each other and designed to carry out operations provided by the concession agreement), the title to which belongs or will belong to the other party (a grantor, public partner), (ii) to conduct business using (operating) the object of the concession agreement, and the grantor undertakes to grant to the concessionary a right to use and hold the object of the concession agreement for the term provided therein for the purposes of conducting of the said activity (BTO, i.e. 'build-transfer-operate' model).

Until recently such concession model did not permit the grantor (public partner) to pay for the range of works/services provided by the concessionary, that prevented the parties from entering into so called *life cycle contracts*[2], especially important for those investment projects provided free of charge for final users (construction of free roads, social healthcare facilities, penal facilities, *etc.*). Life cycle contracts permit to payback the investments contributed by the private partner not by means of tariffs set with respect to final consumers, but rather by means of periodical payments effectuated by the public partner for so-called 'operational availability' ('availability payments') which is twice important from for effective usage of budgetary funds. Federal Law No. 265-FZ of 21 July 2014 amended the Concession Law permitting the grantor to pay to concessionary, and cleared the way for LCC projects on a wide range of infrastructure forms.

It shall be noted that concession agreements in Russia are entered into in accordance with exemplary agreements being approved by the Russian Government for the purposes of each possible object of concession agreement[3]. Concession agreements shall contain material terms and conditions set out by the Concession Law, other federal laws and may contain those terms and conditions that are not governed by the said exemplary agreements to the extent permitted by the Russian legislation and tender documents.

General private legal disadvantages of Russian legislation governing concession agreements include minimum number of the permitted forms of concession (possibility to create concessions only of BTO (build-transfer-operate) and DBFO/DBFM (life cycle contracts) type which do not provide, for example, that ownership title to the object may arise or can be acquired by the private partner), lack of flexibility

---

2   LCC, also known as turnkey contracts, DBFO (design-build-finance-operate) contracts, DBFM (design-build-finance-maintain contracts, PFI (private finance initiative) contracts.

3   By its legal nature a Model Concession Agreement should be deemed as a regulation which together with the Concession Law constitutes a regulatory framework for entering into a specific concession agreement. Using of Model Agreements constitutes an additional guarantee of rights to the parties to PPP. If a Model Agreement contains any provisions infringing on the rights of private investors (for example, unlawfully restrict access to projects, contain onerous terms, *etc.*) such provisions shall be recognized as void by court.

and discretion with respect to terms and conditions of concession agreements (including mandatory nature of exemplary concession agreements), the closed list of admissible PPP objects (not including such infrastructure objects like social welfare facilities, social housing, state and municipal administration facilities), the absence of a wide range of guarantees for the private investor, the fact that norms related to pledge and change of party to the obligation are insufficiently adapted to concession model, the absence of proper mechanism for the implementation of private initiative in PPP projects (unrequested proposals are provided for, but there are no provisions on compensation for investor's expenses occurred during project preparation, he does not get any benefits when competing for the project prepared by him, etc.), insufficient adaptation of tax and budget legislation, *etc.* At the same time it should be noted that the PPP regulation was significantly advanced in 2014. In addition to expanding the range of permitted PPP models (owing to life cycle contracts),

* the possibility to pledge rights under a concession agreement (to raise funds for the project) was expressly provided;
* the possibility to enter into agreements directly with financing organisations (it used to be possible with respect to motorways only) was provided;
* the private partner's priority to buy out the property being a part of the object of the concession agreement upon the expiry thereof (under privatisation procedure) was provided;
* the possibility of joint participation of grantors (several public partners involved in the project) was arranged, guarantees to the private partner were expanded (detailed regulation of the grounds of and procedure for changing of the material terms and conditions of the concession agreement upon request of the private partner, the possibility to prolong the period of compensation for the private partner's expenses up to 2 years, limitation of the grounds for termination of the concession agreement at the initiative of the grantor, more detailed regulation of so-called "grandfather clause" (a guarantee to the private partner in the event of any regulations aggravating its position), etc.).

It should be also noted that the amendments made to the Law on Concession Agreements in summer, 2014 (some of them are to become effective on 1 March and 1 May, 2015) are aimed to broadly satisfy the interested persons (above all, public and private partners as well as financing organizations), requiring adequate tools for PPP projects realisation and, consequently, to reduce the interest to the project of the Federal Law 238827-6 On the Fundamentals of Public

Private Partnership in the Russian Federation which was widely discussed. Despite the fact that the said draft law became, at a lapse of three years of work on it, quite clear and well-elaborated, meeting the key global PPP standards, it was not substantially supported by the federal authorities (the Administration of the President of the Russian Federation, the Ministry of Finance, the Federal Antimonopoly Service) who continue considering public procurement as the principal public private partnership model in the sphere of infrastructure.

In principle, taking into account the amendments made, the current concession legislation allows structuring most of concession and PPP (Life Cycle) projects based on public property to infrastructure. Essentially, in the present form the Law on Concession Agreements, including the both key PPP tools (concession and Life Cycle), looks like a PPP law, rather than a concession law. However, the Federal PPP Law is still necessary and vital; the draft law is still being discussed in the State Duma of the Russian Federation and the enactment thereof in 2015-2016 is not unlikely.

Regional Legislation

There is an attempt to eliminate the abovementioned disadvantages of the federal regulation of PPP, for example to the extent related to the range of possible PPP forms, closed list of admissible PPP objects as well as to necessary discretion, etc. by means of regional laws. As of the beginning of 2015 more than 4/5 of the Russian constituent territories (almost 70 regions) adopted special laws on private-public partnerships elaborated, mostly, on the basis of the **Regional Model Law "On Participation of a Constituent Territory of the Russian Federation, Municipality in Public-Private Partnership Projects"** approved on 22 April, 2009 by the Expert Council on Public-Private Partnership Legislation with the Committee for Economic Policy and Business of the State Duma of the Russian parliament (below referred to as the "**Regional Model PPP Law**") as well as the highly successful experience of the Law of St. Petersburg dated 25.12.2006 N 627-100 "On participation of St. Petersburg in public-private partnerships".

This model law (article 5) suggests expanding of the range of PPP forms to be used in Russia through introducing a BOT/ROT (build/reconstruct-operate-transfer) and DBOT/DROT (design-build/reconstruct-operate-transfer) models at the regional level. The private partner may preserve an ownership title to the object upon completion of the final phase of performance under PPP agreement ((D)BOO – "(design)-build-own-operate" model), as well as to use PPP in other forms provided by the regional regulations subject to requirements of the federal laws. For example in St. Petersburg Law No. 627-100 "On Participation of Saint-Petersburg in Public-Private Partnerships" of 25 December, 2006 deemed to be one of the most advanced regional PPP laws permits application of "Build & Transfer" and "Operation & Maintenance" models in addition to the mentioned concession model and BOT/ROT, DBOT/DROT and BOO models proposed by the model law.

Application of the said provisions of the model law and additional PPP forms established by regional laws is connected with the general problem of PPP regulation at the regional level. The problem is that according to article 71 of the Russian Constitution as well as to par. 1 article 3 of the Russian Civil Code civil legislation falls within the competence of the federal legislature. Therefore, any regulations issued by the regions and municipalities governing civil law relations between a public and private party shall be deemed void. That is why the problems of civil law regulations of the PPP relations (e.g. allowed PPP forms in private law, rights and obligations of the parties to PPP, allocation of civil legal risks, *etc.*) are unlikely to be resolved by virtue of a regional initiative.

However, such an initiative seems quite beneficial: for example, from the perspective of express provision of the terms and conditions, possibilities, guarantees and procedures not covered by civil law or not prohibited by legislation, *i.e.* falling within the principle of discretion. If the regional initiative is implemented correctly upon application of PPP regulation, such provisions can contribute to legal certainty, transparency and protection of competition in PPP area.

Unification of PPP legislation in CIS countries

On 28 November 2014 during the session of the Interparliamentary Assembly of the Commonwealth of Independent States (CIS) the Model PPP Law for the CIS Member States has been approved. This law was prepared upon request of the Interparliamentary Assembly by a working group consisting of scientists and practitioners representing the Law Faculty of Saint Petersburg State University, namely Vladimir F. Popondopulo as a head of the working group (professor, head of commercial law department of the Law Faculty), Natalia A. Sheveleva (professor, dean of the Law Faculty) and other respected professionals, including Vladimir Kilinkarov and Elena Kilinkarova (partner of Maxima Legal, senior researcher with the Law Faculty and counsel of Maxima Legal, associate professor with the Law Faculty, respectively). The authors of this model PPP law tried to take into account recommendations of international institutes and organizations as well as experience of PPP regulation of the leading economies and those countries where PPP laws are adopted and effective. Experts of European Bank for Reconstruction and Development as well as a number of large international law firms specialized in PPP participated in discussion. It helped to make the law adapted as much as possible to the needs of the partners, funding organizations and all the PPP projects participants.

We hope that this progressive document elaborated on the basis of best liberal practices and proposing a balance of interests of private and public partners and financing organizations, will allow solving many problems related to legal regulation of PPP in Russia and CIS countries. At the same time it will be just an advisory document of harmonization nature that can be used by any country, including Russia in course of development and reforming of its PPP regulations.

Intellectual Property

* by Vladimir Kilinkarov

The provisions of Russian intellectual property law are based on the generally recognized principles and norms of international law and international treaties on intellectual property to which Russia is a party, including:

- the Berne Convention on the Protection of Literary and Artistic Works (1886);
- the Paris Convention on the Protection of Industrial Property (1883);
- the Universal (Geneva) Copyright Convention (1952);
- the International (Rome) Convention on the Protection of the Rights of Performers, Phonogram Producers and Broadcasting Organizations (1961);
- the Geneva Convention on the Protection of Phonogram Producers against the Unauthorized Reproduction of Their Phonograms (1971);
- The Singapore Treaty on the Law of Trademarks (2006).

A recent wide-ranging reform of the legislation on intellectual property resulted in the summarization of norms set forth in separate intellectual property laws in the fourth part of the RF Civil Code, enacted on 1 January 2008.

Pursuant to Article 1225 of the RF Civil Code, the following intellectual property (results of intellectual activity) and means of individualization are protected in Russia:

1) scientific, literary and artistic works;
2) computer programs;
3) databases;
4) performances;
5) phonograms;
6) broadcasting on air or by cable of radio or TV programs (broadcasting of on-air or cable broadcasting companies);
7) inventions;

8) utility models;
9) industrial designs;
10) selection achievements;
11) integrated microcircuit topologies;
12) production secrets (know-how);
13) company names;
14) trade and service marks;
15) names of places of origin of commodities;
16) commercial titles.

State Registration of Intellectual Property

In general, the exclusive right to intellectual property or means of individualization is recognized and protected in the Russian Federation on the grounds of the very fact of their creation. In events provided for in the RF Civil Code the exclusive right to intellectual property or means of individualization is recognized and protected subject to the state registration of such property or means. In particular, the following are subject to state registration:

* inventions;
* utility models;
* industrial designs;
* selection achievements;
* integrated microcircuit topologies;
* trade and service marks;
* names of places of origin of commodities.

A right-holder is obliged to notify the Federal Executive Authority on Intellectual Property of any and all modifications of data relating to the state registration of the results of intellectual activity (means of individualization). In the event of such obligation not being fulfilled, the risks of adverse consequences shall be transferred to the right-holder.

In cases where, in accordance with the RF Civil Code, the result of intellectual activity or means of individualization is subject to state registration, the alienation of the exclusive right to such property or means under an agreement, the pledge of such right and provision of right to use such property or means under the agreement and the transfer of the exclusive right to such property or such means shall also be subject to state registration, the procedure and terms of which are established by the Government of the Russian Federation. The Russian Civil Code clearly defines the list of documents to be submitted and information to be indicated in an application needed to complete the registration of an agreement. Failure to comply with these requirements leads to the following: the transfer of the exclusive right, its pledge or the right to use it are considered to be canceled.

State registration of the alienation of the exclusive right to intellectual property or means of individualization, state registration of the pledge of such right and state registration of the provision of the right to use such property or means under the agreement shall be effected by means of registration of the corresponding agreement. A breach of this requirement shall lead to the invalidity of the agreement.

Intellectual Property Transactions

The right-holder may dispose of his/her right to intellectual property or means of individualization in any way that does not contradict the law and the essence of such exclusive right, including by means of its alienation by agreement in favor of another person (exclusive right alienation agreement) or by providing another person with the right to use the respective intellectual property or means of individualization within the limits specified in the agreement (licensing agreement). Entering into a licensing agreement does not imply the transfer of the exclusive right to the license holder.

An agreement which does not expressly indicate that the exclusive right to intellectual property or means of individualization is to be transferred in full shall be regarded as a licensing agreement, with the exception of an agreement concluded in respect of the right to use intellectual property especially created or to be created for the purposes of its inclusion in a complex object.

The transfer of the exclusive right to intellectual property or means of individualization to another person without entering into an agreement with the right-holder is permitted in the cases and on the grounds stipulated by law, including by way of universal succession (inheritance, reorganization of a legal entity) and in the event of enforcement of the property of the right-holder.

Exclusive Right Alienation Agreement

Pursuant to an exclusive right assignment agreement, one party (the right-holder) shall transfer or pledge to transfer its exclusive right to intellectual property or means of individualization in full to the other party (the transferee).

The exclusive right alienation agreement shall be executed in writing and shall be subject to state registration in the aforementioned cases. Failure to execute such an agreement in writing or the requirement for the state registration thereof shall lead to the agreement being considered null and void.

Pursuant to an exclusive right alienation agreement, the transferee undertakes to pay the remuneration specified therein to the right-holder, unless the agreement expressly specifies its gratuitousness. In the absence of a specified amount of remuneration or procedure for its calculation in a non-gratuitous exclusive right alienation agreement, that agreement shall be considered non-concluded.

As a general rule non-repayable alienation of exclusive rights in relationships between business organizations it is not allowed.

The exclusive right to intellectual property or means of individualization shall be transferred from the right-holder to the transferee at the moment of execution of the exclusive right alienation agreement, unless the parties have agreed otherwise. If the exclusive right alienation agreement is subject to state registration, the exclusive right to intellectual property or means of individualization shall be transferred from the right-holder to the transferee at the moment of state registration of the agreement.

Licensing Agreement

Under a licensing agreement, one party – the holder of the exclusive right to intellectual property or means of individualization (the licenser) – shall provide or undertake to provide the other party (the licensee) with the right to use such intellectual property or means of individualization within the limits specified in the agreement. The licensee may use the intellectual property or means of individualization only within the limits of such rights and by such means as are provided for in the licensing agreement. The right to use intellectual property or means of individualization that is not expressly specified in the licensing agreement shall not be considered to have been granted to the licensee.

A licensing agreement may contain following provisions:

1) the licensee is entitled to use the intellectual property or means of individualization and the licenser reserves the right to grant licenses to other persons (an ordinary (non-exclusive) license);

2) the licensee is entitled to use the intellectual property or means of individualization and the licenser does not reserve the right to grant licenses to other persons (an exclusive license).

Unless otherwise specified in the licensing agreement, the license is deemed to be ordinary (non-exclusive).

As with an alienation agreement, a licensing agreement shall be executed in writing and shall be subject to state registration in the aforementioned cases. Failure to execute such an agreement in writing or the requirement for the state registration thereof shall lead to the agreement being considered null and void.

A licensing agreement shall contain a provision indicating the area in which it is permitted to use the intellectual property or means of individualization. If the agreement contains no provision indicating the area in which it is permitted to use the intellectual property or means of individualization, the licensee shall be entitled to use them on the entire territory of the Russian Federation.

The period of a licensing agreement's validity may not exceed the term of the exclusive right to the intellectual property or means of individualization. In a case where no period of validity is specified in a licensing agreement, the agreement shall be considered as having been entered into for a period of five years, unless otherwise stated in the RF Civil Code. In the event of the termination of the exclusive right, the licensing agreement shall be rescinded.

As with an exclusive right alienation agreement, a licensing agreement is, as a rule, non-gratuitous. In the absence of provision for the amount of remuneration or the procedure for its calculation in a non-gratuitous licensing agreement, that agreement shall be considered as being non-concluded.

A licensing agreement must specify:

1) the subject of the agreement by means of an indication of the intellectual property or means of individualization, the right to the use of which is to be granted under the agreement, as well as specifying, as appropriate, the number and date of issue of the document certifying the exclusive right to the property or means (patent, certificate);
2) the methods of using the intellectual property or means of individualization.

The transfer of the non-exclusive right to intellectual property or means of individualization to a new right-holder shall not be grounds for the modification or termination of the licensing agreement entered into with the previous right-holder.

With the written consent of the licenser the licensee may grant the right to use the intellectual property or means of individualization under the agreement to another person (a sublicensing agreement).

Patent Attorneys

An applicant, a right-holder or other interested party may interact with the federal executive body independently or via a patent attorney registered with the said federal body, or via another representative.

Citizens permanently residing outside the Russian Federation and foreign legal entities may interact with the federal executive body for intellectual property only via patent attorneys registered with the said federal body, unless otherwise specified by international treaties to which the Russian Federation is a party.

The authority of a patent attorney or other representative shall be confirmed by a power of attorney.

Any citizen of the Russian Federation permanently residing in Russia may be registered as a patent attorney. Further requirements to a patent attorney and his/her authority to conduct affairs relating to the legal protection of intellectual property or means of individualization shall be established by law.

Creation of a Specialized Court for Intellectual Property Rights

The **Court for Intellectual Property Rights** which is the first Russian specialized arbitration court was formed in the Russian Federation in 2013.

The Code of Arbitration Procedure of the Russian Federation determines the **jurisdiction** of the Court for Intellectual Property Rights. For example, as the first instance court the Court for Intellectual Property Rights considers:

1) those cases related to the **challenging of normative acts issued by the federal executive authorities** that involve the rights and lawful interests of an applicant in the sphere of legal protection of the results of intellectual activity and means of individualization;

2) cases on disputes related to the provision or termination of legal protection of the results of intellectual activity and means of individualization of legal entities equivalent to them, including products, works, services and undertakings (with the exception of objects of copyright and related rights, semiconductor topography rights).

All other disputes related to intellectual property are to be referred to arbitration courts and courts of general jurisdiction in compliance with their respective jurisdiction and competence. The Court for Intellectual Property Rights shall also consider cases as a court of cassation and review decrees adopted by it (including those that have entered into legal force) in the light of new and newly discovered circumstances. Decisions of the first instance may not be appealed.

Employment

* by Vladimir Kilinkarov, Natalia Zelentsova

The principal source of employment law in Russia is the RF Labor Code No. 197-FZ of 30 December 2001.

The purpose of employment law is to establish state guarantees of citizens' labor rights and liberties, to create favorable working conditions, and to protect the rights and interests of employers and employees.

Russian employment legislation is based on the generally recognized principles and provisions of international law and the fundamental principles of legal regulation of labor relations and other relations directly associated with them as set out in the Constitution of the Russian Federation.

The RF Constitution declares freedom of employment and the right of each individual to manage his/her own capacity to work, to choose a type of activity and profession. In exercising this right a citizen enters into labor relations, the parties to which are the **employee** (an individual, normally over 16) and the **employer** (an individual or a legal entity). Those considered as employers are individuals who are registered as individual entrepreneurs and conduct business without forming a legal entity, private notaries, barristers who have founded legal offices, and other persons whose professional activity is subject to state registration and (or) licensing pursuant to federal laws; and individuals who have entered into labor relations with employees for personal service and housekeeping assistance.

The regulation of labor relations and other relations directly associated with them may be implemented by means of the conclusion, modification and amendment of collective agreements, contracts and employment agreements between employers and employees; these agreements may not contain provisions restricting the rights or reducing the level of guarantees of employees under labor legislation. Employers (excluding employing individuals who are not individual entrepreneurs) issue local normative acts containing labor law provisions (hereinafter referred to as "local normative acts") within the scope of their competence in accordance with labor law and other legal acts containing provisions of labor law, collective agreements and contracts.

The maintenance of human resources documentation in Russian companies is called **personnel records** and is a fairly complicated procedure involving the drawing-up by a specialist of various documents that are mandatory under employment law (orders, resolutions, regulations, instructions, agreements, contracts, schedules, time sheets *etc.*). The absence of these documents may in some cases entail administrative liability for an organization and other adverse consequences.

Labor relations are relations based on an agreement between an employee and an employer (**employment agreement**) concerning the personal performance of a labor function (work in a job in accordance with the staff list, profession, speciality with a specified qualification; the specific kind of work the employee is charged with) for remuneration. The employee shall be obliged to observe internal labor regulations and the employer shall be obliged to ensure labor conditions provided for by labor law and other legal acts containing provisions of labor law, collective agreement, contracts, local legal acts and the employment agreement. The Labor Code regulates in detail the entire scope of rights and obligations of both employees and employers.

Social Partnerships in the Labor Sphere

A social partnership in the labor sphere means a system of relations between employees (representatives of employees), employers (representatives of employers), state authorities, local government authorities focusing on ensuring the coordination of interests of employees and employers in respect of regulation of labor relations and other relations directly associated with them.

There are several levels of social partnership: federal, interregional, regional, branch, territorial and local.

The following types of social partnership should be highlighted: collective negotiations related to the drafting of collective agreements and contracts and the conclusion of collective agreements; mutual consultations (negotiations) on the regulation of labor relations and other relations directly associated with them, the ensuring of guarantees of employees' labor rights and the improvement of labor legislation and other legal acts containing provisions of labor law; the participation of employees or their representatives in the management of an organization; the participation of representatives of employees and employers in the resolution of labor disputes.

Employees are represented in social partnerships by trade unions, associations or other representatives elected by the employees. The employer is represented by the company executive, an individual entrepreneur in person or his/her authorized representatives. The organs of a social partnership are commissions for the regulation of social and labor relations. Employees also have the right to participate in the management of an organization directly or through their representative bodies in forms established by law.

Employment Agreement

When a citizen is employed, the employee and employer enter into an agreement (employment agreement), under which the employer undertakes to provide the employee with work in accordance with a stipulated labor function, to ensure the established working conditions and to pay the employee's salary on time and in full; the employee undertakes to perform the labor function specified in the agreement personally and to observe the employer's current internal labor regulations. The Labor Code provides for specific guarantees in the event of entering into an employment agreement; the terms of the agreement may be modified by agreement of the parties. An employment agreement may be terminated at any time upon the mutual agreement of the parties thereto. An employee is entitled to terminate his/her employment agreement unilaterally with two weeks prior written notice to his employer; an employer may terminate the agreement only in cases expressly provided for by law. Russian labor legislation provides for the mandatory participation of the elective body of the primary trade union organization in consideration of issues relating to the termination of an employment agreement on the initiative of the employer.

Working Time and Time Off

As far as **working time** is concerned, it may not exceed 40 hours per week. Reduced working time, part-time working and overtime is established for some categories of employees. The RF Constitution guarantees each person the **right to time off**. The duration of working time, days off and public holidays, and a paid annual vacation are guaranteed for an employee working under an employment agreement pursuant to federal law. During a working day (shift) an employee shall be provided with breaks for rest and meals for a period of no more two hours and no less than 30 minutes. The duration of the weekly uninterrupted rest period may be not less than 42 hours. All employees shall be provided with days off and public holidays. It is expressly prohibited to engage employees for work on such days, besides in exceptional cases. Employees shall be granted annual vacations for a period of 28 calendar days, with their employment and average salary preserved.

Salary

Salary of an employee depends on his/her qualifications, the complexity of the work performed, the quantity and quality of labor input, and has no maximum limit. However, a minimum salary is established for the entire territory of the Russian Federation by federal law: it may not be lower than the minimum subsistence level for an employable person. An employee's salary shall be determined by the employment agreement in accordance with the employer's current remuneration systems. A higher salary is paid for working in particular conditions (for employees engaged in arduous work or under harmful and dangerous conditions). Such harmful and dangerous working conditions are identified during a special procedure - a special working conditions assessment.

Special Working Conditions Assessment

A special assessment of working conditions is a set of measures on the identification of hazardous and harmful factors of industrial environment and labor process aimed at assessment of their impact on employees. The employer is obliged to carry out such an assessment together with the special organizations assessing working conditions, with the funding of such assessment carried out by the employer. After completion of the assessment the employer is obliged to acquaint employees with its results, as well as put the data on its website. For violation of the established procedure of the special assessment of working conditions the employer may be held administratively liable.

Labor Discipline

An employer shall be obliged to create the necessary conditions for employees to observe labor discipline. Labor regulations in an organization shall be determined by internal labor regulations. An employer shall encourage employees who carry out their duties conscientiously (by expressing gratitude, issuing a bonus, awarding a valuable gift or a certificate of honor, or by recommending employees for the title of best in their profession). For committing a disciplinary offense, *i.e.* the non-performance or improper performance through the employee's fault of employment duties imposed on him/her, an employer has the right to impose disciplinary penalties: a reprimand, reproof, or dismissal on the appropriate grounds. As a general rule an employer may independently determine the necessity of professional training or retraining required for his/her own needs. However, in cases stipulated by federal laws and other legal acts, professional training of employees (auditors, railway workers, etc.) is the responsibility of the employer.

Damage Liability

A party to an employment agreement bears **damage liability** and is obliged to compensate for damage caused to the other party. The damage liability of the parties may be specified in writing in the employment agreement or annexes thereto. The contractual liability of the employer before the employee may not be lower, and contractual liability of the employee to the employer may not be higher, than that provided for by the Labor Code or other federal laws.

The employer shall bear full liability for damage caused to the employee in full; the employee, however, bears liability only for direct actual damage caused to the employer (loss of profits is not subject to penalty) and only within the limits of his/her average monthly salary, unless otherwise provided for by the RF Labor Code or other federal laws. The employee is obliged to compensate the employer in full for direct actual damage in the case of a shortage of valuables entrusted to him/her on the basis of a special written agreement or committed to him/her under a one-time document in the event of: willful damage; damage caused in a state of alcoholic, drug-induced or other toxic intoxication; damage caused as the result of criminal action by the employee or as the result of an administrative offense; in the case of the disclosure of information constituting a secret protected by law; in the event of causing damage not in the course of performance of his employment duties, and in certain other cases including when an agreement on full individual or collective liability is entered into (permissible only in respect of certain occupations and types of work) between the employee and employer.

The executive of a company shall be fully liable for direct actual damage caused to the company, but in cases provided for in appropriate employment agreements the deputy executive and the chief accountant of the company may also bear such liability.

Protection of Labor Rights and Liberties

Each person is entitled to protect his/her labor rights and liberties by any means not prohibited by law. The principal measures for the protection of labor rights and liberties are: self-protection of labor rights by employees; protection of the labor rights and lawful interests of employees by trade unions; state supervision and control over the observance of labor legislation and other legal acts containing provisions of labor law; judicial protection.

State control is exercised over the observance of labor legislation and other legal acts containing provisions of labor law by all employers in Russia by means of federal labor inspection. In addition, trade unions are entitled to control the observance of labor law and other legal acts containing provisions of labor law, fulfillment of the conditions of collective agreements and contracts. Besides that, a citizen who employs a method of self-protection of his/her labor rights may, with prior written notice to his/her employer or immediate supervisor or other representative of the employer, refuse to perform work not specified in the employment agreement or work that directly threatens his/her life and health.

There are labor disputes commissions in Russia, engaged in the consideration of individual labor disputes between employees and employers on matters of the application of labor legislation and other legal acts containing provisions of labor law, collective agreements, contracts, local legal acts and employment agreements. Such disputes are also considered by the courts. With respect to collective disputes in connection with the institution and amendment of working conditions, the conclusion, amendments and carrying out of collective agreements and contracts, and also in connection with situations where the employer refuses to take into account the opinion of an elected representative body of employees in the course of the adoption of local legal acts, such disputes are considered and resolved within the framework of conciliation procedures.

In accordance with the RF Constitution, employees have the right to strike as a means of resolving a collective labor dispute.

A strike is a temporary voluntary refusal of employees to carry out their employment duties (entirely or in part) in order to resolve a collective labor dispute.

Liability for a Breach of Labor Law

The Labor Code provides for liability for a breach of labor legislation and other acts containing provisions of labor law. Persons guilty of a breach of labor legislation and other acts containing provisions of labor law shall be held disciplinarily and financially liable in accordance with the procedure set out in the Labor Code and other federal laws and shall be called to account for civil, administrative and criminal liability under the procedure set out in federal laws.

Taxation

* by Elena Kilinkarova

Russian Tax System: general overview

Under the Constitution of the Russian Federation everyone shall be obliged to pay the legally established taxes and fees.

The following taxes are currently imposed in the Russian Federation:

A. Federal Taxes:

 1) corporate income tax;
 2) individual income tax;
 3) value added tax;
 4) excises;
 5) mineral extraction tax;
 6) water tax.

B. Regional Taxes:

 1) corporate property tax;
 2) transport tax;
 3) gambling industry tax.

C. Local Taxes:

 1) land tax;
 2) individual property tax.

Russian taxes are grouped into federal, regional and local taxes in accordance with allocation of taxing rights among federal government, regional governments and local authorities. Federal taxes are imposed on the entire territory of the Russian Federation by the RF Tax Code. Regional taxes are imposed by the RF Tax Code and by the regional laws on the territory of the respective region of the Russian Federation. Local taxes are imposed by the RF Tax Code and by the local acts on the territory of the respective municipality. In Moscow, St. Petersburg and Sevastopol local taxes are imposed not by the local authorities but by the city government (that is by the regional authorities). Therefore, definition of tax liability should be based not only on the analysis of the federal tax legislation (mainly the RF Tax Code) but also regional legislation and local acts in respect to regional and local taxes.

Together with federal, regional and local taxes Russian tax system includes special tax regimes under which several taxes (usually VAT, income and property taxes) are replaced by a single payment. The RF Tax Code currently imposes five special tax regimes:

1) unified agricultural tax;
2) simplified tax system;
3) imputed income tax;
4) production sharing agreement tax system;
5) patent based simplified tax system.

According to the RF Tax Code tax is a compulsory individual contribution with no certain benefit received in return. Alongside with taxes Russian legislation imposes fees that are compulsory contributions tied to the contributor's receipt of a benefit as a result of public services. Fees may be imposed by the RF Tax Code (for example stamp duty, sales duty, biological resources use fee) and other federal laws. Fees imposed by the RF Tax Code need not correspond precisely to the value of the benefit, while other fees are expected to be equivalent in value to the service rendered.

The RF Tax Code defines taxpayers as legal entities and individuals liable to pay tax according to the Code. Branches and representative offices of the company are not considered to be an independent taxpayer.

Russian tax legislation uses division of legal entities into Russian and foreign organizations on the basis of a formal incorporation criterion:

* Russian organizations are legal entities incorporated in accordance with Russian legislation;
* foreign organizations are legal entities, companies and other corporate entities with civil legal capacity incorporated in accordance with legislation of a foreign state, international organizations as well as established in Russia branches and representative offices of the mentioned legal entities and international organizations.

Rules of tax assessment may vary greatly for Russian and foreign organizations, especially in respect of definition of the object of taxation and way of assessment (for example, self-assessment vs withholding).

Since 1st of January 2015 the RF Tax Code uses one more tax sensitive concept - a concept of tax resident in respect to legal entities – previously it was used only for individuals. The introduced concept of tax residency of legal entities is rather complicated and is based on the test of the place of management.

The organizations recognized as tax residents of the Russian Federation are all Russian organizations as well as foreign organizations with place of effective management in the Russian Federation. With regard to foreign entities an exception to the general rule may be provided by an international treaty. Exclusively for the purposes of the application of an international treaty foreign organization may be regarded as a tax resident of the Russian Federation according to another criterion on the basis of the provisions of the relevant international tax treaty.

The RF Tax Code thoroughly identifies when the Russian Federation is recognized to be a place of management of the foreign organization. In particular, the Russian Federation will be regarded as a place of management of the foreign organization if at least one of the following conditions is fulfilled:

- executive body regularly carries out its activities in relation to this organization from the territory of the Russian Federation;
- persons authorized and responsible for planning, directing and controlling the activities of the company mainly carry out their activities in the form of governing management of the foreign organization in the Russian Federation.

In some cases place of bookkeeping or managerial accounting of the organization, place of office work and place of staff operational management may be important for the recognition of foreign organization as a tax resident of the Russian Federation.

At the end of the brief overview of the rules determining tax residency of the organizations it should be noted that the new rules for determining the tax residency of the organizations are quite complex and are not limited to the above mentioned provisions.

Most taxpayers pay taxes individually. However the RF Tax Code gives affiliated Russian organizations that meet necessary requirements (including 90% ownership of the parent company) an opportunity to establish a consolidated group of taxpayers for the purposes of tax assessment for corporate income tax in order to take into account the overall economic results of the group operation despite of existence of formally separate corporate entities.

In most cases Russian organizations and individual entrepreneurs pay taxes on the basis of self-assessment. Tax rules differ greatly for foreign organizations depending on whether foreign organization operates in the Russian Federation through permanent establishment or doesn't operate in the Russian Federation through permanent establishment but receives income from the sources in the Russian Federation. Usually foreign organizations that operate in the Russian Federation through permanent establishment pay taxes on the basis of self-assessment, while foreign organizations with no permanent establishment in the Russian Federation pay taxes on income from the sources in the Russian Federation on withholding basis.

Taxes are to be paid after the end of the tax period, which can be a calendar month, a quarter or a year. Usually organizations are obliged to file a tax return after the expiration of the tax period. Together with tax period for some taxes special reporting periods are introduced (usually when the tax period is a calendar year, reporting periods are the first, second and third quarters) with taxpayer being obliged to pay advance payments and file a return after the expiration of the reporting period.

General and special anti-avoidance rules

Russia doesn't have a statutory general anti-avoidance rule (GAAR) and the concept of the limits of permissible tax optimization mostly rests upon application of legal views of the Supreme Commercial Court of the Russian Federation (highest instance for commercial courts in Russia till 06 August 2014) set out in the decree of the Plenum of the Supreme Commercial Court N 53 of 12 October 2006.

According to the Supreme Commercial Court position the taxpayer has the right to reduce his tax burden by any lawful means. The Court thoroughly defines criteria of tax evasion based on business purpose, economic substance and substance over form doctrines. The main criteria to justify tax benefit are that the tax benefit is obtained in the course of real entrepreneurial or other economic activity and there is any independent business purpose for this activity apart from tax benefit. If profits are made solely or mostly of tax benefit and there is no intention to carry out real economic activity, the taxes are levied according to the real economic substance of taxpayers' activity.

As for the special anti-avoidance rules (SAARs) the Russian legislation contains basic SAARs, in particular, transfer pricing rules, thin capitalization rules, controlled foreign companies rules.

Corporate Income Tax

Russian organizations and foreign organizations that operate in Russia through permanent establishment or receive income from sources in Russia are liable to pay corporate income tax.

The object of taxation is taxpayers' profit with different concepts of profit being applicable to Russian and foreign organizations. For Russian organizations "profits" means income minus expenses. For foreign organizations the definition of "profits" depends on whether the foreign organization operates in Russia through its permanent establishment or merely receives income from the sources in Russia. For foreign organization that operates in Russia through permanent establishment profit is defined as income of the permanent establishment minus expenses of the permanent establishment. For foreign companies that only receive income from the sourced in Russia profit consists only of the received income with no deduction of any expenses.

As a general rule every income incurred in a business context is taxable and every expense incurred in a business context is deductible if it is economically justified and documented. However as corporate income taxation is very schedular in Russia there are a lot of special provisions about taxation of certain types of income and expenses.

Basic tax rate is 20%. Some types of income are taxed at rate of 0%, 9%, 10%, 15% and 30%.

The tax period is one calendar year. Along with the tax period, on the expiration of which a payment of the total tax amount shall be made and a tax return shall be filed, two types of reporting periods are established: 1) first quarter, half-year and nine-month periods of a calendar year and 2) each month of a calendar year. Taxpayers shall pay advance payments and file returns based on the results of the reporting periods.

Corporate income tax is paid on the basis of self-assessment with exception made for foreign organizations that only receive income form the sources in the Russian Federation and don't have a permanent establishment in the Russian Federation. For these foreign organizations corporate income tax is paid through withholding at the source of income.

Value Added Tax (VAT)

Organizations (both Russian and foreign), individual entrepreneurs and persons recognized as VAT taxpayers in connection with the transfer of goods across the customs border of the Customs Union are taxpayers of VAT.

The following operations shall be subject to VAT:

* sale of goods, works and services in Russia and the transfer of property rights;
* transfer of goods, works and services in Russia for one's own needs, which are not deductible in corporate income tax;
* construction and installation works for one's own needs;
* import of goods to the territory of the Russian Federation or other territories under its jurisdiction.

The RF Tax Code contains an extensive list of operations not subject to VAT and operations exempt from VAT.

The tax period is one quarter.

Basic tax rate is 18%, reduced rates are 0 % (for example, for the export of goods) and 10% (for example, for the sale of food products, products for children and medical products).

Taxpayers pay VAT on the basis of self-assessment with special rules being applicable to foreign organizations. Foreign organizations with several subdivisions in Russia may choose one subdivision to pay tax and file returns on all transactions of all subdivisions. If a foreign organization is not registered as a taxpayer of VAT the tax is withheld by the person who is the source of payment and is registered as a taxpayer of VAT (usually a Russian organization or individual entrepreneur).

Other Taxes Paid by Organizations

Excises

Organizations (both Russian and foreign) and individual entrepreneurs performing operations regarded as object of taxation as well as persons recognized as taxpayers in connection with the transfer of goods across the customs border of the Customs Union are considered to be excise taxpayers. The list of taxable operations is extensive with sale of excisable goods (for example, alcoholic beverages, tobacco products, petroleum products and automobiles) in Russia being one of the main taxable events. The tax period is one month. Rates are determined for each type of excisable goods.

Corporate Property Tax

Russian and foreign organizations are taxpayers of corporate property tax if they own assets which are identified as taxable objects. For example, foreign organizations operating in Russia through permanent establishment are liable to pay tax if they own immovable and movable assets recorded in the balance sheet as fixed assets and assets received under concession agreements. Those foreign organizations that don't operate in Russia through permanent establishment are liable to pay tax only if they own immovable assets in Russia or have received these assets under the concession agreement.

The RF Tax Code contains the list of taxable objects that includes land and other nature objects (for example, water objects), federal cultural heritage objects (monuments of history and culture) of the peoples of the Russian Federation, ships registered in the Russian International Register of Vessels, icebreakers, nuclear power vessels and atomic and technology service vessels, space crafts and some other assets.

The tax period is one calendar year. The first quarter, six months and nine months of a calendar year are defined by the RF Tax Code as reporting periods, however regional parliament has right to establish no reporting periods.

The tax rate is imposed by regional parliament and the basic rate may not exceed 2.2%.

Transport Tax

Organizations (both Russian and foreign) and individuals are taxpayers of transport tax if they own taxable assets – cars, motorcycles, buses, other self-propelled vehicles, pneumatic and tracked mechanisms, water craft and aircraft, excluding those expressly listed in the RF Tax Code.

The tax period is one calendar year. The first quarter, six months and nine months of a calendar year are defined by the RF Tax Code as reporting periods, however regional parliament has right to establish no reporting periods.

The tax rate is imposed by regional parliament on the basis of the RF Tax Code provisions.

Land tax

Russian and foreign organizations and individuals are taxpayers of land tax if they own taxable assets – land plots with some types of land plots being excluded from the list of taxable assets (for example, land plots that are excluded or restricted in civil circulation, some land plots from forest and state owned water funds). Tax base is a cadastral value of the lands as at 1st of January of the taxable year.

The tax period is one calendar year. The first quarter, six months and nine months of a calendar year are defined by the RF Tax Code as reporting periods, however local authorities (as well as Moscow, St. Petersburg and Sevastopol) have the right to establish no reporting periods.

The tax rate is imposed by the local authorities (as well as Moscow, St. Petersburg and Sevastopol) on the basis of the RF Tax Code provisions.

Please visit official site of the Russian Federal Tax Service - *www.nalog.ru*.

Customs Regulation

* by Elena Kilinkarova

The Russian Federation and regional economic integration

The Russian Federation is an active participant of regional economic integration. On the basis of negotiations and existing international agreements of 1994-1999 the Treaty on the Establishment of the Eurasian Economic Community (EurAsEC) was signed on 10 October 2000 in Astana and came into force on 30 May 2001 after its ratification by all member states.

According to the Treaty the Eurasian Economic Community is an international organization created to effectively advance process of the formation by the contracting states of the Customs Union and the Common Economic Space and to achieve other objectives and purposes laid down in the Agreement on the Customs Union of 6 January 1995 and 20 January 1995, the Treaty on Increased Integration in the Economic and Humanitarian Fields of 29 March 1996 and the Treaty of the Customs Union and the Common Economic Space of 26 February 1999 in accordance with the phases outlined in those documents. Five states have been members of the Eurasian Economic Community from its formation -
Belarus, Kazakhstan, Kyrgyzstan, Russia and Tajikistan.

In accordance with the statutory aims and objectives of the Community and governed by the principle of multispeed integration, in 2007 to 2010 Belarus, Kazakhstan and Russia created the Customs Union and started to form the next stage of integration – the EurAsEC Common Economic Space.

The Resolution on Establishment of the EurAsEC Customs Union was adopted by the heads of six Community states at a EurAsEC Interstate Council meeting on 6 October 2007. At the same time it was determined that at the initial stage the Customs Union shall be formed by three Community countries – Belarus, Kazakhstan and Russia, and that other EurAsEC members should join only at a time when their economies and legislative systems are ready.

The Customs Union is a form of trade and economic integration between the parties, envisaging a common customs territory in the confines of which goods exchanged in mutual trade that originated from the common customs territory and also those originating from third countries and freely circulating on this customs territory are exempt from customs duties and restrictions of an economic nature, apart from special protective, anti-dumping and compensatory measures. Meanwhile the parties apply a unified customs tariff and other unified measures for regulating goods trading with third countries. As distinct from the previous stage of integration – the free trade zone – the Customs Union presupposes free movement on the common customs territory not only of goods produced therein, but also of those from third countries freely circulated in the territory. The supreme body of the Customs Union is the Interstate Council at the level of heads of states and heads of governments, and a unified permanent regulatory body of the union is the Customs Union Commission.

Customs regulation in the Customs Union is carried out according to the customs legislation of the union, and in the part which isn't regulated by such legislation according to the legislation of member states of the Customs Union.

The customs legislation of the union includes the Customs Code of the Customs Union (the Treaty on the Customs Code of the Customs Union No. 17 dated 27 November 2009 is adopted by the Decision of the Interstate Council of the Eurasian Economic Community (the supreme body of the Customs Union) at the level of heads of states), international treaties of member states and decisions of the Customs Union Commission. In the Russian Federation the Customs Code of the Customs Union (hereinafter – CC of the Customs Union, CUCC) is applied since 1 July 2010. Thus, at present provisions of the CC of the Customs Union have direct application, and the Customs Code of the Russian Federation until recalled is applied insofar as it does not conflict with the CC of the Customs Union.

In December 2009 at an informal summit in Almaty the presidents of Belarus, Kazakhstan and Russia approved the Plan of Action for 2010-2011 on forming a Common Economic Space (CES) comprised of the three countries. It envisages the drawing up and signing by 1 January 2012 of twenty international treaties to enable the establishment of the CES.

The last for today stage of regional economic integration started when the Treaty on the Eurasian Economic Union (EAEU) was signed on 29 May 2014 by Belarus, Kazakhstan and Russia. The treaty became effective on the territory of the Russian Federation on 1 January 2015. The treaty is based on the legal framework of the Customs Union and the Common Economic Space that was optimized, improved and brought into accordance with rules of the World Trade Organization.

The Eurasian Economic Union (hereinafter - Union, EAEU) is an international organization of regional economic integration that provides free movement of goods, services, capital and labor and pursues coordinated, harmonized and single policy in the sectors of economy determined by the EAEU Treaty and international treaties within the Union.

Main purposes of EAEU are:

- to arrange conditions for stable development of economies of member states in interests of increasing a standard of living of the population;
- to strive for creation of the common market of goods, services, capital and labor within the Union;
- overall modernization, cooperation and increase of competitiveness of national economies in the conditions of global economy.

According to the article 32 of the Treaty on the Eurasian Economic Union, the Customs Code of the Eurasian Economic Union, international treaties and other acts that form the law of EAEU provide common customs regulation within EAEU.

Customs Clearance

All commodities and vehicles crossing the customs border of the Customs Union are subject to customs clearance and customs control. As a general rule, customs clearance shall be conducted in the place of location of customs bodies during their regular working hours.

Commodities imported into the customs territory of the Customs Union shall be under customs control from the moment of crossing the customs border. Termination of customs control may be caused by the actual export of commodities from the customs territory of the Customs Union, the application of customs procedures related to release of commodities for domestic consumption, and a number of other circumstances.

Customs control involves the checking of documents and information, an oral examination, obtaining explanations, customs supervision, customs inspection, customs examination, customs checks, and certain other procedures.

Declaration of Commodities

As a general rule, when commodities cross the border, and also in the event of a change in the customs regime, commodities shall be subject to declaration to customs bodies. The customs declaration may be made in written or electronic form. Depending on the published customs procedures and the persons transporting commodities, the following types of customs declaration shall apply: commodity declaration, transit declaration, passenger customs declaration and vehicle declaration.

Declaration of commodities shall be made either by the customs declarant or by a customs representative acting on behalf of the customs declarant. Subject to certain terms and conditions, both citizens of the Customs Union member states and foreign individuals and legal entities may act as customs declarants. A legal entity incorporated in a member state of the Customs Union and included in the Register of Customs Representatives may act as a customs representative. Relations between the customs declarant and the customs representative shall be based on a contract.

In the customs declaration commodities shall be classified pursuant to the Foreign Trade Commodity Nomenclature (see Decision of the Eurasian Economic Commission No. 54 of 16 July 2012 "On Approval of the Uniform Foreign Trade Commodity Nomenclature of the Customs Union and the Unified Customs Tariff"). The customs authorities shall verify whether commodities have been classified correctly. In the event of the incorrect classification of commodities, the customs authority shall independently classify them and decide upon the classification of commodities in compliance with the format provided for by the legislation of the Customs Union member states. Decisions of the customs authorities are subject to appeal.

As a general rule, customs declarations relating to the import of commodities shall be filed prior to expiration of the temporary storage period (usually two months) and declarations relating to the export of commodities – before they leave the customs territory of the Customs Union.

Customs Payments

According to Article 70 of the CUCC, the following payments constitute customs payments: import customs duty, export customs duty, value added tax and excise levied on the import of commodities into the customs territory of the Customs Union, as well as customs duties for customs clearance, customs escort and storage.

Customs duties rates consist of the following types (Article 71 of the CUCC):

1) ad valorem - set as a percentage of the customs value of the commodities on which they are imposed;
2) specific - set in accordance with physical characteristics on the basis of quantities (quantity, mass, volume or other characteristics);
3) combined - combining the types specified in items 1) and 2).

Commodities transported across the customs border shall be subject to customs duties. Depending on the type of commodity and the applicable rates, the customs value of commodities and/or their physical characteristics on the basis of quantities (quantity, mass inclusive of the original package inseparable from commodity prior to its consumption in which such commodity is delivered for retail, volume or other characteristics) shall be the base for the calculation of customs duties. However, the taxable base shall be determined pursuant to the legislation of the Customs Union member states (Article 75 of the CUCC).

There are different ways of paying customs charges, depending on the customs procedures applied. The Customs Code of the Customs Union provides for 17 customs procedures (Article 20265 of the CUCC), including: release for domestic consumption, export, customs warehouse, re-import, re-export and temporary import (export).

As a general rule, the customs declarant shall be the payer of the customs payments and he/she shall calculate the amount to be paid. A customs declarant or a customs representative acting for and on behalf of a declarant shall be held liable for providing false information in the customs declaration or failing to fulfill obligations stipulated by the CUCC in observance of the conditions and requirements of the customs procedure (Articles 65, 189 and 207 of the CUCC). It should be noted that in accordance with Article 186 of the CUCC, regardless of the terms and conditions of a foreign trade transaction, a person from the Customs Union member state which consummated such transaction shall be deemed a declarant, and he or she (not a foreign contractor) shall be liable for breach of the customs regulations.

Customs duties and taxes shall be paid (imposed) in that Customs Union member state whose customs body releases the commodities, with the exception of commodities released under the customs procedure of transit or on the territory of which illegal transportation across the customs border has been determined (Article 84 of the CUCC). Customs payments shall be payable in the currency of the Customs Union member state in which they are to be paid.

Russian legislation provides for advance payments in the form of funds credited to the accounts of the Federal Treasury towards future customs payments, not identified by the payer as specific types, and sums of customs payments relating to specific commodities (Article 73 of the CUCC). Such funds are considered as the property of the person making the advance payment and may not be regarded as customs payments until that person makes a statement to the customs body or the customs body levies execution upon such funds.

Judiciary System

* by Natalia Zelentsova

In the Russian Federation judicial power is exercised only by courts. It is independent and acts separately from the legislative and executive branches. Judicial power is exercised by means of constitutional, civil, administrative and criminal legal procedures. In the Russian Federation justice may be administered only by courts established in accordance with the Constitution of the Russian Federation and Federal Constitutional Law "On the Judiciary System of the Russian Federation" No. 1-FKZ of 31 December, 1996. It is impermissible to form emergency courts or courts not provided for by the above law.

The Russian Federation judiciary system consists of **three judiciary system branches**:

1. A system of constitutional courts consisting of the Constitutional Court of the Russian Federation and the constitutional (charter) courts of constituent territories of the Russian Federation. The Constitutional Court of the Russian Federation is not the superior body of the constitutional (charter) courts of constituent territories of the Russian Federation.

2. A system of courts of general jurisdiction consisting of justices of the peace, district courts and garrison military courts, the supreme courts of constituent territories of the Russian Federation and circuit (navy) military courts and the Supreme Court of the Russian Federation.

3. A system of national 'arbitrazh courts' (not arbitration but national commercial courts, hereinafter referred to as the "commercial courts") consisting of commercial courts of constituent territories of the Russian Federation, district commercial courts (commercial courts of cassation) and the Supreme Court of the Russian Federation. A specialized Court for Intellectual Property Rights operates within the system of commercial courts.

It should be noted that previously system of commercial courts was headed by the Supreme Commercial Court of the Russian Federation. However, it was abolished, and ceased its activity from 6 August, 2014. At the moment, the highest judicial body for civil cases, cases on economic disputes, criminal, administrative and other cases under the jurisdiction of the courts formed in accordance with the Federal Constitutional Law "On the Judicial System of the Russian Federation" and the federal laws, is the Supreme Court of the Russian Federation.

The judicial system consists of federal courts and courts of the constituent territories of the Russian Federation. The latter include constitutional (charter) courts and justices of the peace of the constituent territories of the Russian Federation. The rest of the foregoing courts are federal as they are created and funded at federal level.

A court ruling that has entered into legal force, or lawful instructions, demands, orders, summons and other communications of court **are binding throughout** the Russian Federation for any and all persons. Failure to abide by a court ruling or other contempt of court shall entail liability set out in the legislation of the Russian Federation.

In compliance with the principle of publicity, proceedings in all courts are public. Hearings in camera are permitted only in cases provided for by federal law (for example, if public proceedings may lead to disclosure of a legally protected secret).

Proceedings in the Constitutional Court of the Russian Federation, the Supreme Court of the Russian Federation and other commercial and military courts shall be held in Russian. Proceedings in other courts may also be held in the national language of the republic where the court is located. The parties to the proceedings that do not speak the language of the proceedings shall be entitled to speak or furnish explanations in their native language or in any other freely chosen language for communication and to engage an interpreter.

Jurisdiction

The Constitutional Court of the Russian Federation has jurisdiction over the compliance of federal laws, regulations issued by the President of the Russian Federation and the Government of the Russian Federation, as well as the constitutions (charters) and laws of constituent territories of the Russian Federation, with the Constitution of the Russian Federation. In addition, the Constitutional Court of the Russian Federation provides the official interpretation of the Constitution of the Russian Federation. Constitutional (charter) courts of the constituent territories of the Russian Federation check compliance of the regulations of a constituent territory of the Russian Federation with the constitution (charter) of such constituent territory of the Russian Federation and the interpretation thereof.

Commercial courts have jurisdiction over economic disputes and other cases relating to the conducting of entrepreneurial or other economic activities. In general, two criteria exist on the basis of which one may determine whether commercial court has jurisdiction over a case: 1) the economic nature of the dispute, 2) the specific parties (legal entities and individual entrepreneurs). Although the latter criterion is not determinative, it still serves as supplementary to the criterion of the nature of the dispute.

In those cases that fall within the special jurisdiction of a commercial court it is irrelevant whether legal entities or individuals are the parties to the proceedings. Insolvency (bankruptcy) cases, corporate disputes, disputes on protection of good standing in economic activity and some other cases come within this special jurisdiction. Disputes on the protection of intellectual property rights also come under the special jurisdiction of commercial courts.

Commercial courts consider cases on challenging the non-legislative acts, decisions, actions and omissions of authorities and officials if they affect the rights and interests of an applicant in the area of entrepreneurial and other economic activities. These courts also consider cases on challenging the legislative acts of federal executive bodies in the field of patent rights and rights to selection achievements, topographies of integrated circuits, trade secrets (know-how), means of individualization of legal entities, goods, services and enterprises, rights to use the results of intellectual activity in the integrated technology.

Courts of general jurisdiction consider cases which do not fall within the jurisdiction of commercial courts (specifically, those cases in which one of the parties is a citizen who does not carry out entrepreneurial activity, unless such a case is referred to the special jurisdiction of a commercial court). Courts of general jurisdiction consider cases involving citizens and cases involving legal entities that are not of an economic nature. Cases on challenging regulations pursuant to complaints by citizens and organizations are considered by courts of general jurisdiction, unless such cases are referred to the jurisdiction of other courts. Challenges to the decisions, actions and omissions of officials and authorities are based on citizens' complaints. Complaints of legal entities and citizens acting as entrepreneurs shall be accepted if the challenged act breaches their rights and lawful interests not related to economic activity.

System of Courts of General Jurisdiction

Courts of general jurisdiction consider criminal, administrative and civil cases.

A system of military courts stands apart in the system of courts of general jurisdiction. Military courts are formed on an area basis and exercise judicial power among troops, bodies and commands where military service is provided by law. The system of military courts consists of garrison military courts and circuit (navy) military courts.

In other respects, the system of courts of general jurisdiction consists of justices of the peace, district courts and the supreme courts of constituent territories of the Russian Federation.

The authority of the foregoing courts is strictly demarcated by the federal law. The authority of justices of the peace, the supreme court of a constituent territory of the Russian Federation and the Supreme Court of the Russian Federation are determined separately. The competence of a district court is determined on the leftover principle.

The justice of the peace is the first instance for a specific category of cases. The district court considers cases as the court of the first and appeals instance and is superior to the justice of the peace. The supreme court of a constituent territory of the Russian Federation also considers specific categories of cases as the court of the first, appeals and cassation instance and is superior to the district courts of a constituent territory of the Russian Federation.

System of Commercial Courts

In commercial courts justice is administrated in observance of general principles of publicity, the language of proceedings, equality before the law and the court and the binding nature of judicial acts.

The main objectives of commercial courts when they try disputes are: protection of the breached or disputed rights and lawful interests of enterprises, institutions, organizations and individuals in the area of entrepreneurial or other economic activities and provision of assistance in consolidation of law and prevention of a breach of the law in the said area.

The system of commercial courts in the Russian Federation consists of: commercial courts of the first instance in a constituent territory of the Russian Federation, commercial courts of appeal and district commercial courts (commercial courts of cassation). A specialized court operates in the system of commercial courts. It is the Court for Intellectual Property Rights.

The authority of commercial courts is strictly demarcated by federal law. With reference to the specific category of a case, the competence of district commercial court, commercial court of appeal and specialized court is determined. The competence of a commercial court of the first instance is determined on the leftover principle.

Within the framework of the appeal procedure commercial courts of appeal verify the legality and reasonableness of awards made by commercial courts of a constituent territory of the Russian Federation that have not yet come into legal force. All an all there are 21 commercial court of appeal in the Russian Federation.

Within the framework of the cassation procedure a district commercial court verifies the legality and reasonableness of awards made in cases considered by the commercial court of a constituent territory of the Russian Federation and commercial courts of appeal that have already come into legal force. This court is competent to try some categories of cases as the court of the first instance.

The Court for Intellectual Property Rights is a specialized commercial court which commenced operation in 2013. It tries specific categories of cases related to disputes involving the protection of intellectual property rights falling within its competence as a court of the first and cassation instances. In particular, as a court of the first instance the Court for Intellectual Property Rights considers cases on determining patent holder, invalidation of patent, early termination of legal protection of trademark if it is not used, *etc.* Those disputes that do not come within the jurisdiction of the Court for Intellectual Property Rights expressly set out in law shall be tried by other commercial courts and courts of general jurisdiction. For more details on the Court for Intellectual Property Rights, please see the *Intellectual Property* section.

Supreme Court of the Russian Federation

The Supreme Court of the Russian Federation consists of the following Judicial Divisions (Chambers): the Division for Administrative Cases, the Division for Civil Cases, the Division for Criminal Cases, the Division for Economic Disputes and the Military Division. The said Judicial Divisions consider cases as courts of the first, as well as appeal and cassation instance. The Appeal Division and the Disciplinary Division are also formed under the aegis of the Supreme Court. The Appeal Division considers cases, which were previously considered in first instance by the Judicial Divisions as a court of second (appellate) instance as well as cases due to new or newly discovered facts. The Disciplinary Division considers cases on challenge of certain decisions of the High Qualification Board of Judges of the Russian Federation. The structure of the Supreme Court of the Russian Federation contains the Presidium of the Supreme Court which reviews judgments that came into legal force by way of judicial supervision. The Presidium is entitled to review specific matters of court practice and inform lower-level courts of the results of such review. The receipt of such information is crucial to ensure uniformity of court practice. Another structural element of the Supreme Court is its Plenum, which is entitled to clarify issues related to the implementation of legislation in order to ensure uniformity of court practice. These clarifications are binding for the system of courts of general jurisdiction and commercial courts and exercise a significant influence over the formation of court practice.

Constitutional Proceedings

Constitutional proceedings are exercised in the Constitutional Court of the Russian Federation and the constitutional (charter) courts of constituent territories of the Russian Federation. Within the framework of constitutional proceedings only matters of law are resolved, i.e. factual background is not investigated if it falls within the competence of other courts. Constitutional proceedings are based on the principle of the independence, publicity, collective and adversarial nature of the proceedings and the equality of the parties to the proceedings.

Constitutional proceedings may be initiated upon applications by governmental authorities or a court, if the disputable regulation applies to a specific case tried in that court. These proceedings may be initiated by complaints from individuals or legal entities if disputable regulation applies or is applicable to their case.

A decision of the Constitutional Court of the Russian Federation is final and binding. It has direct effect and is not subject to approval by other governmental authorities. Those acts that are recognized as unconstitutional shall become void. The Constitutional Court of the Russian Federation is the only body entitled to interpret the provisions of the Constitution of the Russian Federation. Legal views expressed by it shall be binding thought the Russian Federation for any and all persons.

Civil and Arbitration Proceedings

Civil proceedings are carried out by courts of general jurisdiction and commercial courts depending on their jurisdiction. The main regulations governing civil proceedings are the Code of Civil Procedure of the Russian Federation and the Code of Arbitration Procedure of the Russian Federation (hereinafter referred to as the "**RF APC**"). Civil and arbitration proceedings are regulated at federal level only and are based on similar principles and norms (the term "arbitration proceedings" refer to proceeding in the national commercial courts herein and does not refer to arbitration proceedings).

Civil proceedings and arbitration proceedings focus on the legitimate and timely consideration and resolution of civil cases in order to protect the breached or disputed rights, freedoms and lawful interests of individuals, organizations, the rights and interests of the Russian Federation, constituent territories of the Russian Federation, municipalities or other persons acting as parties to civil, labor or other legal relations. Civil and arbitration proceedings are carried out in observance of the principles of equality before the law and the court, the independence of judges, publicity, the language of the proceedings, the binding nature of judicial acts and administration of justice based on the adversarial nature of proceedings and the equality of the parties to the proceedings.

In civil and arbitration proceedings citizens may participate in the proceedings in person or by proxy. If a citizen participates in proceedings in person, he will not be divested of his right to have a proxy in the case. Organizations are represented in court by bodies acting within the powers in which they have been vested or by other representatives of the organization.

In civil proceedings the evidence in the case is information on facts obtained in compliance with the procedure provided by law based on which the court determines whether or not there are circumstances serving as grounds for demands or objections of the parties to the proceedings and other circumstances important for the legitimate review and resolution of the case. Such information may be obtained through explanations of the parties to the proceedings or of third parties, witness testimonies, written or physical evidence, audio and video records and expert opinions. The list is exhaustive. Evidence obtained in breach of the law shall be invalid and may not be assumed as a basis for a court decision. Each party to the proceedings bears a burden on proof in respect of the evidence it provides as the grounds for its demands and objections.

Within the framework of civil proceedings, in both courts of general jurisdiction and commercial courts the following types of proceedings exist: action proceedings, writ proceedings, proceedings on cases arising out of public legal relations and special proceedings.

The only type of proceedings characterized by the existence of an issue in law between equal parties is action proceedings. Action proceedings focus on resolving such issues.

Writ proceedings are indefeasible, *i.e.* under such proceedings no dispute is presumed and they involve issuance of an enforceable writ by the court.

Under proceedings on cases arising out of public legal relations the regulations, decisions, actions or omissions of governmental authorities and officials are disputed. In these proceedings the court determines whether the disputed acts are lawful and if it adjudicates that a disputable act is not in compliance with law, one of the following decisions shall be made. If a regulation is disputed, it will be declared ineffective; if a decision, action or omission of governmental authority or official is disputed, the court will oblige such authority or official to remedy the violation committed.

Under special proceedings the court determines facts that have legal implications. In addition, cases on insolvency (bankruptcy) and some other categories of cases are considered under special proceedings.

It should be noted that the new Code of Administrative Procedure of the Russian Federation will come into force from 15 September, 2015. This Code will regulate administrative proceedings when considering the following administrative cases by the Supreme Court of the Russian Federation and courts of general jurisdiction: cases on defense of violated or disputed human rights, freedoms and legitimate interests, rights and legitimate interests of the organizations as well as other administrative cases resulted from administrative and other public legal relationships related to judicial control of legality and validity of exercising of state and other public authority.

Proceedings on Cases Involving Foreign Nationals (Entities)

Foreign nationals, stateless persons, foreign entities and international organizations are entitled to apply to courts of the Russian Federation to seek protection of their breached or disputed rights. Foreign parties enjoy the same procedural rights and fulfill the same procedural duties as Russian citizens and organizations.

The standing of foreign nationals in court in civil proceedings, their legal capacity and the capacity of foreign entities to sue shall be governed by their personal law. The personal law of a foreign national or a foreign entity means the law of the country whose citizenship such national possesses or where such entity was incorporated. However, a foreign national or a foreign entity lacking legal capacity or capacity to sue under the personal law may be recognized as having the foregoing capacities in compliance with Russian law.

The law contains a list of situations where courts of the Russian Federation are entitled to try cases involving foreign nationals and entities (specifically, when the respondent is located in the Russian Federation or if the suit arises out of an agreement performed or to be performed In the Russian Federation in full or in part or if the parties entered into the agreement on referring disputes to a Russian arbitration court, *etc.*). The law includes an exhaustive list of cases involving foreign nationals and entities to be considered solely by courts of the Russian Federation. For example, cases on disputes arising out of transportation agreements, if the carriers are located in the Russian Federation, or cases on disputes on title to real estate located in the Russian Federation.

Enforcement of Court Decisions

As soon as a judicial act enters into effect, a writ of execution shall be issued to the execution creditor. In accordance with Federal Law "On Enforcement Proceedings" No. 229-FZ of 2 October 2007, upon application of the execution creditor an enforcement officer initiates enforcement proceedings on the basis of the enforcement document. The execution officer is entitled to sequester the debtor's property to have the claims of the execution creditor fulfilled or introduce other restrictions. The enforcement officer may apply enforcement measures in order to fulfill such claims. Claims of the execution creditor shall be satisfied out of the debtor's property. However, the law provides for some kinds of property which may not be sequestered: for example, private belongings, with the exception of luxury items. As soon as the claims set out in the enforcement document are actually satisfied, enforcement proceedings shall be terminated.

Administrative Proceedings

Administrative proceedings are carried out in courts of general jurisdiction and commercial courts. The main regulations governing administrative proceedings are the Code of Administrative Offenses of the Russian Federation (hereinafter referred to as the "**RF AOC**") and the RF APC.

The law distinguishes the competence of courts of general jurisdiction from that of commercial courts. In the commercial court system administrative proceedings are governed by the RF APC, though in the system of courts of general jurisdiction they are governed by the RF AOC.

Proceedings on cases relating to administrative offenses focus on the comprehensive, complete and timely investigation of the factual background of each case, resolving it in compliance with the law, ensuring enforcement of the ruling made and discovering the grounds and conditions that facilitated the administrative offenses to be committed.

Unlike in civil proceedings, in administrative proceedings there is a presumption of innocence: it is presumed that the respondent is innocent of the offense and is not obliged to prove his innocence.

Criminal proceedings

Criminal proceedings may be carried out only in courts of general jurisdiction. The main regulations governing criminal proceedings are the Code of Criminal Procedures of the Russian Federation.

Criminal proceedings aimed at the protection of the rights and lawful interests of individuals and organizations who are victims of crime; protection of a person from unlawful and unsubstantiated charges, conviction, restriction of the person's rights and freedoms. The fundamental principles of criminal proceedings in the Russian Federation are the following: the principle of legality, publicity, administration of justice by court only, defense of rights and freedoms of man and the citizen under criminal proceedings, inviolability of the home, privacy of correspondence, telephone conversations and other communications, presumption of innocence, adversarial nature of proceedings, the language of proceedings, inviolability of the person and respect of the person's honor and dignity, *etc.*

There are two stages of criminal proceedings: pre-trial procedures and trial procedures. Under pre-trial procedures criminal proceedings are instituted and evidence is collected by the prosecution and defense. Under trial procedures the court reviews and resolves criminal cases. Trial procedures may be carried out either as ordinary procedures or as special procedures. Special procedures may be complicated (when a case is considered involving a jury) or simplified (special procedure without court hearings when punishment is mitigated).

Extra-Judicial Dispute Settlement Procedures

Among alternative dispute settlement procedures elaborated in international practice only arbitration proceedings and mediation are enshrined in law in the Russian Federation. Moreover, the latter procedure has only recently been introduced and has not yet become popular.

Arbitration Courts

Arbitration proceedings are an alternative to resolving cases in national courts. The operation of arbitration courts is regulated by Federal Law "On Arbitration Courts in the Russian Federation" No. 102-FZ of 24 July 2002.

A dispute may be referred to an arbitration court only if the parties have entered into an arbitration agreement. An arbitration agreement may be concluded by the parties thereto either in respect of all or specific disputes that have arisen or may arise between the parties in connection with a specific legal relation. An arbitration agreement in the form of an arbitration clause in the agreement shall be deemed several from the other provisions thereof. The conclusion of an arbitration court that an agreement containing an arbitration clause is invalid shall not entail invalidity of the clause by virtue of law. The arbitration court independently resolves whether it is competent or not to try a dispute referred to it.

Arbitration proceedings shall be carried out in observance of the principle of legality, confidentiality, independence and impartiality of arbitrators, permissive rule, the adversarial nature of proceedings and equality of the parties to the proceedings.

There are two types of arbitration courts: permanently operating courts and those formed to resolve a specific dispute. A permanently operating arbitration court carries out proceedings based on permanent rules, while an arbitration court formed to resolve a specific dispute carries out the proceedings based on rules agreed by the parties thereto. Arbitration proceedings shall be held in Russian, unless otherwise agreed by the parties.

Unless the parties have agreed in the arbitration agreement that the arbitration court award shall be binding, a party thereto may appeal it by filing an application to the competent court. An arbitration court award shall be performed voluntarily in accordance with the procedure and within the timelines specified in such an award. If it is not performed voluntarily within the specified timelines, it shall be enforced on the basis of a writ of execution on the enforcement of the arbitration court award issued by the competent court.

International Commercial Arbitration Court

If international commercial arbitration is held in the Russian Federation, Russian Federation Law "On International Commercial Arbitration" No. 5338-1 of 7 July 1993 shall apply.

The parties may agree that the following disputes may be referred to an international commercial arbitration court: disputes under civil law relations arising in connection with foreign trade and other international economic relations, provided that the commercial entity of at least of one of the parties is located abroad, as well as disputes of foreign investment enterprises and international associations and organizations incorporated in the Russian Federation with each other, disputes between their members and disputes with other Russian legal entities.

An arbitration agreement means an agreement of the parties to refer to arbitration any and all disputes that have arisen or may arise between them in connection with any specific legal relation, regardless of whether it was a contract relation or otherwise. An arbitration agreement may be entered into in the form of an arbitration clause in the agreement or in the form of a separate agreement. The clause at issue is several from the other provisions thereof and remains in force if the agreement is deemed void. Like an arbitration court, an international commercial arbitration court independently resolves whether it has competence or not.

An award of an international commercial arbitration court may be appealed by filing a motion for its cancellation with the supreme court of a constituent territory of the Russian Federation. The list of grounds for such cancellation is exhaustive. An award, regardless of the country in which it was made, shall be deemed binding and shall be enforced provided that the respective written motion is filed with the competent court.

There are two permanent international commercial arbitration courts in the Russian Federation: the International Commercial Arbitration Court at the Chamber of Commerce and the Maritime Arbitration Commission at the Chamber of Commerce.

Mediation Procedure

Mediation is a way of resolving disputes on the basis of voluntary consent of the parties aimed at achieving a mutually acceptable decision. The mediation procedure is performed in the Russian Federation by virtue of the Federal Law "On Alternative Dispute Resolution with the Assistance of a Mediator (Mediation Procedure)". This procedure aims at facilitating the development of partnership business relations and ensuring good business conduct.

The mediation procedure is applicable to disputes arising out of civil law relations, including those connected to conducting entrepreneurial and other economic activity, as well as to disputes arising out of labor and family relations. The mediation procedure may be invoked after the dispute has been considered under civil or arbitration proceedings.

The mediation procedure is subject to the mutual will of the parties in observance of the principles of voluntariness, confidentiality, cooperation and equality of the parties to the procedure, as well as the impartiality and independence of the mediator. An agreement to invoke the mediation procedure shall not be an impediment to an application to a court or commercial court, unless otherwise provided by federal law.

The mediator's activity may be conducted on either a professional or an amateur basis. Persons who are eighteen years of age or more, with full legal capacity and no previous convictions, may act as amateur mediators. Persons who hold state posts in the Russian Federation, state posts in the constituent territories of the Russian Federation, state civil service positions or municipal service positions may not act as mediators, unless otherwise stipulated by federal law. Persons who are twenty-five years of age or more, have a higher vocational education and have completed a mediators training program approved in accordance with the procedure set out by the Government of the Russian Federation may act as professional mediators. The mediation procedure relating to disputes referred to a court or commercial court before the mediation procedure was commenced may be carried out only by professional mediators.

Based on the results of mediation, the parties shall enter into a mediation agreement. A mediation agreement shall contain information on the parties thereto, the subject matter of the dispute, the mediation procedure performed and the obligations agreed by the parties, as well as the terms and timelines for their performance. A mediation agreement shall be performed based on the principles of voluntariness and good faith of the parties. A mediation agreement concluded after a dispute has been referred to a court or arbitration court may be adopted as a settlement agreement. A mediation agreement in relation to a dispute arising out of civil law relations reached by the parties under the mediation procedure without referring the dispute to a court or arbitration court shall be deemed a civil law transaction.

Authors list

Maxim Avrashkov, Managing Partner,
Head of General Business Practic, Maxima Legal

Vladimir Kilinkarov, PhD, Partner, Head of the Public-Private
Partnership (PPP) Practice, Head of the International Projects Group,
Maxima Legal

Sergei Bakeshin, Senior Associate, Head of Corporate
and Dispute Resolution Practices, Maxima Legal

Evgeniy Druzhinin, Senior associate, Head of Real Estate
& Construction Practice, Maxima Legal

Elena Kilinkarova, PhD, Counsel
St.Petersburg, Head of Tax Law Practice
Associate professor, Law Faculty, St. Petersburg State University

Natalia Zelentsova, Associate, Maxima Legal

Alina Kozmina, Associate, Maxima Legal

Our Contacts

Maxima Legal LLC

St. Petersburg (head office)   **Moscow**

26, Liteiny Pr., 191028   11, Noviy Arbat Str., 121019
tel/fax: **+7 (812) 454-22-14**   tel/fax: **+7 (495) 665-07-20**
office@maximalegal.ru   officemsk@maximalegal.ru

Welcome to our website www.maximalegal.com

DOING BUSINESS IN RUSSIA
BRIEF LEGAL GUIDE

4th edition

edited by
Vladimir Kilinkarov,
Maxim Avrashkov

St. Petersburg, Russia

2016

Published by RBO Books © 2016
Distributed by Glagoslav Publications Ltd. © 2016